I

ESCAPE

Winston Churchill

first published as
Chapters 5- 11 of
LONDON TO
LADYSMITH VIA
PRETORIA
1900

A CRUISE IN THE ARMOURED TRAIN

Estcourt: November 9, 1899.

How many more letters shall I write you from an unsatisfactory address? Sir George White's Headquarters are scarcely forty miles away, but between them and Estcourt stretches the hostile

army. Whether it may
be possible or wise
to try to pass the
lines of investment
is a question which
I cannot yet decide;
and meanwhile I wait
here at the nearest
post collecting
such information
as dribbles through
native channels,
and hoping that
early events may
clear the road. To
wait is often weary

work—but even at this exciting time I come to a standstill at length with a distinct feeling of relief. The last month has been passed in continual travel. The fading, confused faces at Waterloo as the train swept along the platform; the cheering crowds at Southampton; the rolling decks of the 'Dunottar Castle;'

the suspense, the excitement of first news; a brief day's scurry at Cape Town; the journey to East London by the last train to pass along the frontier; the tumultuous voyage in the 'Umzimvubu' amid so great a gale that but for the Royal Mail the skipper would have put back to port; on without a check to

Pietermaritzburg, and thence, since the need seemed urgent and the traffic slow, by special train here—all moving, restless pictures— and here at last—a pause.

Let us review the situation. On Wednesday last, on November 1, the Boer lines of investment drew round Ladysmith. On Thursday the last train passed down the railway under the fire of artillery. That night the line was cut about four miles north of Colenso. Telegraphic communication also ceased. On Friday Colenso was itself attacked. A heavy gun came into action from the hills which dominate the town, and the slender garrison of infantry volunteers and naval brigade evacuated in a hurry, and, covered to some extent by the armoured train, fell back on Estcourt.

Estcourt is a South African town—that is to say, it is a collection of about three hundred detached stone or corrugated iron houses, nearly all one-storied, arranged along two broad streets—for space is plentiful—or straggling away towards the country. The little place lies in a cup of the hills, which rise in green undulations on all sides. For this reason it will be a very difficult place to defend if the invaders should come upon it. It is, besides, of mean and insignificant aspect; but, like all these towns in Natal, it is the centre of a large agricultural district, at once the market and the storehouse of dozens of prosperous farms scattered about the country, and consequently it possesses more importance than the passing stranger would imagine. Indeed, it was a surprise to find on entering the shops how great a variety and quantity of goods these unpretentious shanties contained.

Estcourt now calls itself 'The Front.' There is another front forty miles away, but that is ringed about by the enemy, and since we live in expectation of attack, with no one but the Boers beyond the outpost line, Estcourt considers that its claim is just, Colonel Wolfe Murray, the officer who commands the lines of communication of the Natal Field Force, hastened up as soon as the news of the attack on Colenso was received to make preparation to check the enemy's advance.

The force at his disposal is not, however, large—two British battalions—the Dublin Fusiliers, who fought at Glencoe, and were hurried out of Ladysmith to strengthen the communications when it became evident that a blockade impended, and the Border Regiment from Malta, a squadron of the Imperial Light Horse, 300 Natal volunteers with 25 cyclists, and a volunteer battery of nine-pounder guns—perhaps 2,000 men in all. With so few it would be quite impossible to hold the long line

of hills necessary
for the protection
of the town, but
a position has
been selected and
fortified, where the
troops can maintain
themselves—at any
rate for several days.
But the confidence
of the military
authorities in the
strength of Estcourt
may be gauged by
the frantic efforts
they are making

to strengthen Pietermaritzburg, seventy-six miles, and even Durban, one hundred and thirty miles further back, by earthworks and naval guns. 'The Boers invade Natal!' exclaims Mr. Labouchere in the number of 'Truth' current out here. 'As likely that the Chinese army should invade London.' But he is not the only false prophet.

It seems, however, certain that a considerable force will be moved here soon to restore the situation and to relieve Ladysmith. Meanwhile we wait, not without anxiety or impatience. The Imperial Horse, a few mounted infantry, the volunteer cyclists, and the armoured train, patrol daily towards Colenso and the north, always expecting to see the approaching Boer commandos. Yesterday I travelled with the armoured train. This armoured train is a very puny specimen, having neither gun nor Maxims, with no roof to its trucks and no shutters to its loopholes, and being in every way inferior to the powerful machines I saw working along the southern frontier. Nevertheless it is a useful means of reconnaissance, nor is a journey in it devoid of interest. An armoured train! The very name sounds strange; a locomotive disguised as a knight-errant; the agent of civilisation in the habiliments of chivalry. Mr. Morley attired as Sir Lancelot would seem scarcely more incongruous. The possibilities of attack added to the keenness of the experience. We started at one o'clock. A company of the Dublin Fusiliers formed the garrison. Half were in the car in front of the engine, half in that behind. Three empty trucks, with a platelaying gang and spare rails to mend the line, followed. The country between Estcourt and Colenso is open, undulating, and grassy. The stations, which occur every four or five miles, are hamlets consisting of half a dozen corrugated iron houses, and perhaps a score of blue gum trees. These little specks of habitation are almost the only marked feature of the landscape, which on all sides spreads in pleasant but monotonous slopes of green. The train maintained a good speed; and, though it stopped repeatedly to question Kaffirs or country folk, and to communicate with the cyclists and other patrols who were scouring the country on the flanks, reached Chieveley, five miles from Colenso, by about three o'clock; and from here the Ladysmith balloon, a brown speck floating above and beyond the distant hills, was plainly visible.

Beyond Chieveley it was necessary to observe more caution. The speed was reduced—the engine walked warily. The railway officials scanned the track, and often before a culvert or bridge was traversed we disembarked and examined it from the ground. At other times long halts were made while the officers swept the horizon and the distant hills with field glasses and telescopes. But the country was clear and the line undamaged, and we continued our slow advance. Presently Colenso came into view—a hundred tin-pot houses under the high hills to the northward. We inspected it deliberately. On a mound beyond the village rose the outline of the sandbag fort constructed by the Naval Brigade. The flagstaff, without the flag, still stood up boldly. But, so far as we could tell, the whole place was deserted.

There followed a discussion. Perhaps

the Boers were lying in wait for the armoured train; perhaps they had trained a gun on some telegraph post, and would fire the moment the engine passed it; or perhaps, again, they were even now breaking the line behind us. Some Kaffirs approached respectfully, saluting. A Natal

Volunteer—one
of the cyclists—
came forward to
interrogate. He was
an intelligent little
man, with a Martini-
Metford rifle, a large
pair of field glasses,
a dainty pair of grey
skin cycling shoes,
and a slouch hat.
He questioned the
natives, and reported
their answers. The
Kaffirs said that
the Dutchmen were

assuredly in the neighbourhood. They had been seen only that morning. 'How many?' The reply was vague—twelve, or seventeen, or one thousand; also they had a gun—or five guns—mounted in the old fort, or on the platform of the station, or on the hill behind the town. At daylight they had shelled

Colenso. 'But why,' we asked, 'should they shell Colenso?' Evidently to make sure of the range of some telegraph post. 'It only takes one shell to do the trick with the engine,' said the captain who commanded. 'Got to hit us first, though,' he added. 'Well, let's get a little bit nearer.'

The electric bell rang three times, and we crept forward—halted—looked around, forward again—halt again—another look round; and so, yard by yard, we approached Colenso. Half a mile away we stopped finally. The officer, taking a sergeant with him, went on towards the village on foot. I followed.

We soon reached the trenches that had been made by the British troops before they evacuated the place. 'Awful rot giving this place up,' said the officer. 'These lines took us a week to dig.' From here Colenso lay exposed about two hundred yards away—a silent, desolate village. The streets were littered with the belongings of the inhabitants. Two or three houses had been burned. A dead horse lay in the road, his four legs sticking stiffly up in the air, his belly swollen. The whole place had evidently been ransacked and plundered by the Boers and the Kaffirs. A few natives loitered near the far end of the street, and one, alarmed at the aspect of the train, waved a white rag on a stick steadily to and fro. But no Dutchmen were to be seen. We made our way back to the railway line and struck it at the spot where it was cut. Two lengths of rails had been lifted up, and, with the sleepers attached to them, flung over the embankment. The broken telegraph wires trailed untidily on the ground. Several of the posts were twisted. But the bridge across the Tugela was uninjured, and the damage to the lines was such as could be easily repaired. The Boers realise the advantage of the railway. At this moment, with their trains all labelled

'To Durban,' they are drawing supplies along it from Pretoria to within six miles of Ladysmith. They had resolved to use it in their further advance, and their confidence in the ultimate issue is shown by the care with which they avoid seriously damaging the permanent way. We had learned all that there was to learn—where the line was broken, that the village was deserted, that the bridge was safe, and we made haste to rejoin the train. Then the engine was reversed, and we withdrew out of range of the hills beyond Colenso at full speed—and some said that the Boers did not fire because they hoped to draw us nearer, and others that there were no Boers within ten miles.

On the way back I talked with the volunteer. He was friendly and communicative. 'Durban Light Infantry,' he said; 'that's my corps. I'm a builder myself by trade—nine men under me. But I had to send them all away when I was called out. I don't know how I'm going on when I get back after it's over. Oh, I'm glad to come. I wish I was in Ladysmith. You see these Dutchmen have come quite far enough into our country. The Imperial Government promised us protection. You've seen what protection

Colenso got; Dundee and Newcastle, just the same; I don't doubt they've tried their best, and I don't blame them; but we want help here badly. I don't hold with a man crying out for help unless he makes a start himself, so I came out. I'm a cyclist. I've got eight medals at home for cycling.'

'How will you like a new one—with the Queen's head on it?'

His eye brightened.

'Ah,' he said, 'I should treasure that more than all the other eight—even more than the twenty-mile championship one.'

So we rattled back to Estcourt through the twilight; and the long car, crowded with

brown-clad soldiers
who sprawled
smoking on the floor
or lounged against
the sides, the rows
of loopholes along
the iron walls, the
black smoke of
the engine bulging
overhead, the sense
of headlong motion,
and the atmosphere
of war made the
volunteer seem
perhaps more than
he was; and I thought

him a true and valiant man, who had come forward in time of trouble quietly and soberly to bear his part in warfare, and who was ready, if necessary, to surrender his humble life in honourably sustaining the quarrel of the State. Nor do I care to correct the impression now.

DISTANT GUNS

Estcourt: November 10, 1899.

When I awoke yesterday morning there was a strange tremor in the air. A gang of platelayers and navvies were making a new siding by the station, and sounds of hammering also came from the engine shed. But this tremor made itself felt above these and all the other noises of a waking camp, a silent thudding, a vibration which scarcely seemed to constitute what is called sound, yet which left an intense impression on the ear. I went outside the tent to listen. Morning had just broken, and the air was still and clear. What little wind there was came from the northwards, from the direction of Ladysmith, and I knew that it carried to Estcourt the sound of distant cannon. When once the sounds had been localised it was possible to examine them more carefully. There were two kinds of reports: one almost a boom, the explosion evidently of some very heavy piece of ordnance; the other only a penetrating whisper, that of ordinary field guns. A heavy cannonade was proceeding. The smaller pieces fired at brief intervals, sometimes three or four shots followed in quick succession. Every few minutes the heavier gun or guns intervened.

What was happening? We could only try to guess, nor do we yet know whether our guesses were right. It seems to me, however, that Sir George White must have made an attack at dawn on some persecuting Boer battery, and so brought on a general action.

Later in the day

we rode out to find some nearer listening point. The whole force was making a reconnaissance towards Colenso, partly for reasons of security, partly to exercise the horses and men. Galloping over the beautiful grassy hills to the north of the town, I soon reached a spot whence the column could be seen.

First of all came
a cyclist—a Natal
volunteer pedalling
leisurely along with
his rifle slung across
his back—then two
more, then about
twenty. Next, after
an interval of a
quarter of a mile,
rode the cavalry—
the squadron of
the Imperial Light
Horse, sixty Natal
Carabineers, a
company of mounted

infantry, and about forty of the Natal mounted police. That is the total cavalry force in Natal, all the rest is bottled up in Ladysmith, and scarcely three hundred horsemen are available for the defence of the colony against a hostile army entirely composed of mounted men. Small were their numbers, but the quality was good. The Imperial Light Horse have shown their courage, and have only to display their discipline to equal advantage to be considered first-class soldiers. The Natal Carabineers are excellent volunteer cavalry: the police an alert and reliable troop. After the horse the foot:

the Dublin Fusiliers wound up the hill like a long brown snake. This is a fine regiment, which distinguished itself at Glencoe, and have since impressed all who have been brought in contact with it. The cheery faces of the Irishmen wore a proud and confident expression. They had seen war. The other battalion—the Border Regiment— had yet their spurs to win. The volunteer battery was sandwiched between the two British battalions, and the rear of the column was brought up by the Durban volunteers. The force, when it had thus passed in review, looked painfully small, and this impression was aggravated by the knowledge of all that depended on it.

A high, flat-topped hill to the north-west promised a wide field of vision and a nearer listening point for the Ladysmith cannonade, which still throbbed and thudded dully. With my two companions I rode towards it, and after an hour's climb reached the summit. The land lay spread before us like a map. Estcourt, indeed, was hidden by its engulfing hills, but Colenso was plainly visible, and the tin roofs of the houses showed in squares and oblongs of pale blue against the brown background of the mountain. Far away to the east the dark serrated range of the Drakensberg rose in a mighty wall. But it was not on these features that we turned our glasses. To the right of Colenso the hills were lower and more broken, and the country behind, though misty and indistinct, was exposed to view. First there was a region of low rocky hills rising in strange confusion and falling away on the further side to a hollow. Above this extensive depression clouds of smoke from grass and other fires hung and drifted, like steam over a cauldron. At the bottom—invisible in spite of our great elevation—stood the town and camp of Ladysmith. Westward rose the long, black, hog-backed outline of Bulwana Hill, and while we watched intently the ghost of a flash stabbed its side and a white patch sprang into existence, spread thinner, and vanished away. 'Long Tom' was at his business.

The owner of the nearest farm joined us while we were

thus engaged—a tall, red-bearded man of grave and intelligent mien. 'They've had heavy fighting this morning,' he said. 'Not since Monday week' (the Black Monday of the war) 'has there been such firing. But they are nearly finished now for the day.' Absorbed by the distant drama, all the more thrilling since its meaning was doubtful and mysterious, we had shown ourselves against the sky-line, and our conversation was now suddenly interrupted. Over the crest of the hill to the rear, two horsemen trotted swiftly into view. A hundred yards away to the left three or four more were dismounting among the rocks. Three other figures appeared on the other side. We were surrounded— but by the Natal Carabineers. 'Got you, I think,' said the sergeant, who now arrived. 'Will you kindly tell us all about who you are?' We introduced ourselves as President Kruger and General Joubert, and presented the farmer as Mr. Schreiner, who had come to a secret conference, and having produced our passes, satisfied the patrol that we were not eligible for capture. The sergeant looked disappointed. 'It took us half an hour to stalk you, but if you had only been Dutchmen we'd have had you fixed up properly.' Indeed, the whole manoeuvre had been neatly and cleverly executed, and showed the smartness and efficiency of these irregular forces in all matters of scouting and reconnaissance. The patrol was then appeased by being photographed 'for the London papers,' and we hastened to accept the farmer's invitation to lunch. 'Only plain fare,' said he, 'but perhaps you are used to roughing it.'

The farm stood in a sheltered angle of the hill at no great distance from its summit. It was a good-sized house, with stone walls and a corrugated iron roof. A few sheds and outhouses surrounded it, four or five blue gums afforded a little shade from the sun and a little relief to the grassy smoothness of the landscape. Two women met us at the door, one the wife, the other, I think, the sister of our host. Neither was young, but their smiling faces showed the invigorating effects of this delicious air. 'These are anxious times,' said the older; 'we hear the cannonading every morning at breakfast. What will come of it all?' Over a most excellent luncheon we discussed many things with these kind people, and spoke of how the nation was this time resolved to make an end of the long quarrel with the Boers, so that there should be no more uncertainty and alarm among loyal subjects of the Queen. 'We have always known,' said the farmer, 'that it must end in war, and I cannot say I am sorry it has come at last. But it falls heavily on us. I am the only man for twenty miles who has not left his farm. Of course we are defenceless here. Any day the Dutchmen may come. They wouldn't kill us, but they would burn or plunder everything, and it's all I've got in the world. Fifteen years have I worked at this place, and I said to myself we may as well stay and face it out, whatever happens.' Indeed, it was an anxious time for such a man. He had bought the ground, built the house, reclaimed waste tracts, enriched the land with corn and cattle, sunk all his capital in the enterprise, and backed it with the best energies of his life. Now everything might be wrecked in an hour by a wandering Boer patrol. And this was happening to a loyal and law-abiding British subject more than a hundred miles within the frontiers of her Majesty's dominions! Now I felt the bitter need for soldiers—thousands of soldiers—so that such a man as this might be assured. With what pride and joy could one have said: 'Work on, the fruits of your industry are safe. Under the strong arm of the Imperial Government your home shall be secure, and if perchance you suffer in the disputes of the Empire the public wealth shall restore your private losses.' But when I recalled the scanty force which alone kept the field, and stood between the enemy and the rest of Natal, I knew the first would be an empty boast, and, remembering what had happened on other occasions, I thought the second might prove a barren promise.

We started on our long ride home, for the afternoon was wearing away and

picket lines are
dangerous at dusk.
The military situation
is without doubt at
this moment most
grave and critical.
We have been at
war three weeks.
The army that was
to have defended
Natal, and was
indeed expected to
repulse the invaders
with terrible loss,
is blockaded and
bombarded in its

fortified camp. At nearly every point along the circle of the frontiers the Boers have advanced and the British retreated. Wherever we have stood we have been surrounded. The losses in the fighting have not been unequal—nor, considering the numbers engaged and the weapons employed, have they been very severe. But the Boers hold more than 1,200 unwounded British prisoners, a number that bears a disgraceful proportion to the casualty lists, and a very unsatisfactory relation to the number of Dutchmen that we have taken. All this is mainly the result of being unready. That we are unready is largely due to those in England who have endeavoured by every means in their power to hamper and obstruct the Government, who have scoffed at the possibility of the Boers becoming the aggressors, and who have represented every precaution for the defence

of the colonies
as a deliberate
provocation to the
Transvaal State.
It is also due to
an extraordinary
under-estimation
of the strength of
the Boers. These
military republics
have been for ten
years cherishing vast
ambitions, and for
five years, enriched
by the gold mines,
they have been

arming and preparing for the struggle. They have neglected nothing, and it is a very remarkable fact that these ignorant peasant communities have had the wisdom and the enterprise to possess themselves of good advisers, and to utilise the best expert opinion in all matters of armament and war.

Their artillery is inferior in numbers, but in nothing else, to ours. Yesterday I visited Colenso in the armoured train. In one of the deserted British-built redoubts I found two boxes of shrapnel shells and charges. The Boers had not troubled to touch them. Their guns were of a later pattern, and fired powder and shell made up together like a great rifle cartridge. The combination, made for the first time in the history of war, of heavy artillery and swarms of mounted infantry is formidable and effective. The enduring courage and confident spirit of the enemy must also excite surprise. In short, we have grossly underrated their fighting powers. Most people in England—I, among them—thought that the Boer ultimatum was an act of despair, that the Dutch would make one fight for their honour, and, once defeated, would accept the inevitable. All I have heard and whatever I have seen out here contradict these false ideas.

Anger, hatred, and the consciousness of military power impelled, the Boers to war. They would rather have fought at their own time—a year or two later—when their preparations were still further advanced, and when the British were, perhaps, involved in other quarters. But, after all, the moment was ripe. Nearly everything was ready, and the whole people sprang to arms with alacrity, firmly believing that they would drive the British into the sea. To that opinion they still adhere. I do not myself share it; but it cannot be denied that it seems less absurd to-day than it did before a shot had been fired.

To return to Estcourt. Here we are passing through a most dangerous period. The garrison is utterly insufficient to resist the Boers; the position wholly indefensible. Indeed, we exist here on sufferance. If the enemy attack, the troops must fall back on Pietermaritzburg, if for no other reason because they are the only force available for the defence of the strong lines now being formed around the chief town. There are so few cavalry outside Ladysmith that the Boers could raid in all directions. All this will have been changed long before this letter reaches you, or I should not send it, but as I write the situation is saved only by what seems to me the over-confidence of the enemy. They are concentrating all their efforts on Ladysmith, and evidently hope to compel its surrender. It may, however, be said with absolute certainty that the place can hold out for a month at the least. How, then, could the Boers obtain the necessary time to reduce it? The reinforcements are on the seas. The railway works regularly with the coast. Even now sidings are being constructed and troop trains prepared. It is with all this that they should interfere, and they are perfectly competent to do so. They could compel us to retreat on Pietermaritzburg, they could tear up the railway, they could blow up the bridges; and by all these means they could delay the arrival of a relieving army, and so have a longer time to worry Ladysmith, and a better chance of making it a second Saratoga. Since Saturday last that has been our fear. Nearly a week has passed and nothing has happened. The chance of the Boers is fleeting; the transports approach the land; scarcely forty-eight hours remain. Yet, as I write, they have done nothing. Why? To some extent I think they have been influenced by the fear of the Tugela

River rising behind their raiding parties, and cutting their line of retreat; to some extent by the serene and confident way in which General Wolfe Murray, placed in a most trying position, has handled his force and maintained by frequent reconnaissance and a determined attitude the appearance of actual strength;

but when all has
been said on these
grounds, the fact
will remain that
the enemy have
not destroyed the
railway because
they do not fear the
reinforcements that
are coming, because
they do not believe
that many will come,
and because they are
sure that, however
many may come,
they will defeat

them. To this end they preserve the line, and watch the bridges as carefully as we do. It is by the railway that they are to be supplied in their march through Natal to the sea. After what they have accomplished it would be foolish to laugh at any of their ambitions, however wicked and extravagant these may be; but it appears to most military critics at this moment that they have committed a serious strategic error, and have thrown away the chance they had almost won. How much that error will cost them will depend on the operations of the relieving force, which I shall hope to chronicle as fully as possible in future letters.

THE FATE OF THE ARMOURED TRAIN

Pretoria: November 20, 1899.

Now I perceive that I was foolish to choose in advance a definite title for these letters and to think that it could continue to be appropriate for any length of time. In the strong stream of war the swimmer is swirled helplessly about hither and thither by the waves, and he can by no means tell where he will come to land, or, indeed, that he may not be overwhelmed in the flood. A week ago I described to you a reconnoitring expedition in the

Estcourt armoured train, and I pointed out the many defects in the construction and the great dangers in the employment of that forlorn military machine. So patent were these to all who concerned themselves in the matter that the train was nicknamed in the camp 'Wilson's death trap.'

On Tuesday, the 14th, the mounted infantry patrols reported that the Boers in small parties were approaching Estcourt from the directions of Weenen and Colenso, and Colonel Long made a reconnaissance in force to ascertain what strength lay behind the advanced scouts. The reconnaissance, which was marked only by an exchange of shots between the patrols, revealed little, but it was generally believed that a considerable portion of the army investing Ladysmith was moving, or was about to move, southwards to attack Estcourt, and endeavour to strike Pietermaritzburg. The movement that we had awaited for ten days impended. Accordingly certain military preparations, which I need not now specify, were made to guard against all contingencies, and at daylight on Wednesday morning another spray of patrols was flung out towards the north and north-west, and the Estcourt armoured train was ordered to reconnoitre towards Chieveley. The train was composed as follows: an ordinary truck, in which was a 7-pounder muzzle-loading gun, served by four sailors from the 'Tartar;' an armoured car fitted with loopholes and held by three sections of a company of the Dublin Fusiliers; the engine and tender, two more armoured cars containing the fourth section of the Fusilier company, one company of the Durban Light Infantry (volunteers), and a small civilian breakdown gang; lastly, another ordinary truck with the tools and materials for repairing the road; in all five wagons, the locomotive, one small gun, and 120 men. Captain Haldane, D.S.O., whom I had formerly known on Sir William Lockhart's staff in the Tirah Expedition, and who was lately recovered from his wound at Elandslaagte, commanded.

We started at half-past five and, observing all the

usual precautions, reached Frere Station in about an hour. Here a small patrol of the Natal police reported that there were no enemy within the next few miles, and that all seemed quiet in the neighbourhood. It was the silence before the storm. Captain Haldane decided to push on cautiously as far as Chieveley, near which place an extensive view of the country could be obtained. Not a sign of the Boers could be seen. The rolling grassy country looked as peaceful and deserted as on former occasions, and we little thought that behind the green undulations scarcely three miles away the leading commandos of a powerful force were riding swiftly forward on their invading path.

All was clear as far as Chieveley, but as the train reached the station I saw about a hundred Boer horsemen cantering southwards about a mile from the railway. Beyond Chieveley a long hill was lined with a row of black spots, showing that our further advance would be disputed. The telegraphist who accompanied the train wired back to Estcourt reporting our safe arrival, and that parties of Boers were to be seen at no great distance, and Colonel Long replied by ordering the train to return to Frere and remain there in observation during the day, watching its safe retreat at nightfall. We proceeded to obey, and were about a mile and three-quarters from Frere when on rounding a corner we saw that a hill which commanded the line at a distance of 600 yards was occupied by the enemy. So after all there would be a fight, for we could not pass this point without coming under fire. The four sailors loaded their gun—an antiquated toy—the soldiers charged their magazines, and the train, which was now in the reverse of the order in which it had started moved, slowly towards the hill.

The moment approached: but no one was much

concerned, for the cars were proof against rifle fire, and this ridge could at the worst be occupied only by some daring patrol of perhaps a score of men. 'Besides,' we said to ourselves, 'they little think we have a gun on board. That will be a nice surprise.'

The Boers held

their fire until the train reached that part of the track nearest to their position. Standing on a box in the rear armoured truck I had an excellent view-through my glasses. The long brown rattling serpent with the rifles bristling from its spotted sides crawled closer to the rocky hillock on

which the scattered
black figures of
the enemy showed
clearly. Suddenly
three wheeled things
appeared on the
crest, and within
a second a bright
flash of light—like a
heliograph, but much
yellower—opened
and shut ten or
twelve times. Then
two much larger
flashes; no smoke nor
yet any sound, and a

bustle and stir among the little figures. So much for the hill. Immediately over the rear truck of the train a huge white ball of smoke sprang into being and tore out into a cone like a comet. Then came, the explosions of the near guns and the nearer shell. The iron sides of the truck tanged with a patter of bullets. There was a crash from the front of the train and half a dozen sharp reports. The Boers had opened fire on us at 600 yards with two large field guns, a Maxim firing small shells in a stream, and from riflemen lying on the ridge. I got down from my box into the cover of the armoured sides of the car without forming any clear thought. Equally involuntarily, it seems that the driver put on full steam, as the enemy had intended. The train leapt forward, ran the gauntlet of the guns, which now filled the air with explosions, swung round the curve of the hill, ran down a steep gradient, and dashed into a huge stone which awaited it on the line at a convenient spot.

To those who were in the rear truck there was only a tremendous shock, a tremendous crash, and a sudden full stop. What happened to the trucks in front of the engine is more interesting. The first, which contained the materials and tools of the breakdown gang and the guard who was watching the line, was flung into the air and fell bottom upwards on the embankment. (I do not know what befell the guard, but it seems probable that he was killed.) The next, an armoured car crowded with the Durban Light Infantry, was carried on twenty yards and thrown over on its side, scattering its occupants in a shower on the ground. The third wedged itself across the track, half on and half off the rails. The rest of the train kept to the metals.

We were not long left in the comparative peace and safety of a railway accident. The Boer guns, swiftly changing their position, re-opened from a distance of 1,300 yards before anyone had got out of the stage of exclamations. The tapping rifle fire spread along the hillside, until it encircled the wreckage on three sides, and a third field gun came into action from some high ground on the opposite side of the line.

To all of this our own poor little gun endeavoured to reply, and the sailors, though exposed in an open truck, succeeded in letting off three rounds before the barrel was struck by a shell, and the trunnions, being smashed, fell altogether out of the carriage.

The armoured truck gave some protection from the bullets, but since any direct shell must pierce it like paper and kill everyone, it seemed almost safer outside, and, wishing to see the extent and nature of the damage, I clambered over the iron shield, and, dropping to the ground, ran along the line to the front of the train. As I passed the engine another shrapnel shell burst immediately, as it seemed, overhead, hurling its contents with a rasping rush through the air. The driver at once sprang out of the cab and ran to the shelter of the overturned trucks. His face was cut open by a splinter, and he complained in bitter futile indignation. He was a civilian. What did they think he was paid for? To be killed by bombshells? Not he. He would not stay another minute. It looked as if his excitement and misery—he was dazed by the blow on his head—would prevent him from working the engine further, and as only he understood the machinery all chances of escape seemed to be cut off. Yet when I told this man that if he continued to stay at his post he would be mentioned for distinguished gallantry in action, he pulled himself together, wiped the blood off his face, climbed back into the cab of his engine, and thereafter during the one-sided combat did his duty bravely and faithfully—so strong is the desire for honour and repute in the human breast.

I reached the overturned portion of the train uninjured. The volunteers who, though severely shaken, were mostly unhurt, were lying down under such cover as the damaged cars and the gutters of the railway line afforded. It was a very grievous sight to see these citizen soldiers, most of whom were the fathers of families, in such a perilous position. They bore themselves well, though greatly troubled, and their major, whose name I have not learned, directed their fire on the enemy; but since these, lying behind the crests of the surrounding hills, were almost invisible I did not expect that it would be very effective.

Having seen this much, I ran along the train to the rear

armoured truck and told Captain Haldane that in my opinion the line might be cleared. We then agreed that he with musketry should keep the enemy's artillery from destroying us, and that I should try to throw the wreckage off the line, so that the engine and the two cars which still remained on the rails might escape.

I am convinced that this arrangement gave us the best possible chance of safety, though at the time it was made the position appeared quite hopeless.

Accordingly Haldane and his Fusiliers began to fire through their loopholes at the Boer artillery, and, as the enemy afterwards admitted, actually disturbed their aim considerably. During the time that these men were firing from the truck four shells passed through the armour, but luckily not one exploded until it had passed out on the further side. Many shells also struck and burst on the outside of their shields,

and these knocked
all the soldiers on
their backs with
the concussion.
Nevertheless a well-
directed fire was
maintained without
cessation.

The task of clearing
the line would not,
perhaps, in ordinary
circumstances
have been a very
difficult one. But
the breakdown gang

and their tools were scattered to the winds, and several had fled along the track or across the fields. Moreover, the enemy's artillery fire was pitiless, continuous, and distracting. The affair had, however, to be carried through.

The first thing to be done was to detach the truck half off

the rails from the one completely so. To do this the engine had to be moved to slacken the strain on the twisted couplings. When these had been released, the next step was to drag the partly derailed truck backwards along the line until it was clear of the other wreckage, and then to throw it bodily off the rails. This may seem very simple, but the dead weight of the iron truck half on the sleepers was enormous, and the engine wheels skidded vainly several times before any hauling power was obtained. At last the truck was drawn sufficiently far back, and I called for volunteers to overturn it from the side while the engine pushed it from the end. It was very evident that these men would be exposed to considerable danger. Twenty were called for, and there was an immediate response. But only nine, including the major of volunteers and four or five of the Dublin Fusiliers, actually stepped out into the open. The attempt was nevertheless successful. The truck heeled further over under their pushing, and, the engine giving a shove at the right moment, it fell off the line and the track was clear. Safety and success appeared in sight together, but disappointment overtook them.

The engine was about six inches wider than the tender, and the corner of its footplate would not pass the corner of the newly overturned truck. It did not seem safe to push very hard, lest the engine should itself be derailed. So time after time the engine moved back a yard or two and shoved forward at the obstruction, and each time moved it a little. But soon it was evident that complications had set in. The newly derailed truck became jammed with that originally off the line, and the more the engine pushed the greater became the block. Volunteers were again called on to assist, but though seven men, two of whom, I think, were wounded, did their best, the attempt was a failure.

Perseverance, however, is a virtue. If the trucks only jammed the tighter for the forward pushing they might be loosened by pulling backwards. Now, however, a new difficulty arose. The coupling chains of the engine would not reach by five or six inches those of the overturned truck. Search was made for a spare link. By a solitary gleam of good luck one was found. The engine hauled at the wreckage, and before the chains parted pulled it about a yard backwards. Now, certainly, the line was clear at last. But again the corner of the footplate jammed with the corner of the truck, and again we came to a jarring halt.

I have had, in the last four years, the advantage, if it be an advantage, of many strange and varied experiences, from which the student of realities might draw profit and instruction. But nothing was so thrilling as this: to wait and struggle among these clanging, rending iron boxes, with the repeated explosions of the shells and the artillery, the noise of the projectiles striking the cars, the hiss as they passed in the air, the grunting and puffing of the engine—poor, tortured thing, hammered by at least a dozen shells, any one of which, by penetrating the boiler, might have made an end of all—the expectation of destruction as a matter of course, the realization of powerlessness, and the alternations of hope and despair— all this for seventy minutes by the clock with only four inches of twisted iron work to make the difference between danger, captivity, and shame on the one hand—safety, freedom, and triumph on the other.

Nothing remained but to continue pounding at the obstructing corner in the hopes that the iron work would gradually be twisted and torn, and thus give free passage. As we pounded so did the enemy. I adjured the driver to be patient and to push gently, for it did not seem right to imperil the slender chance of escape by running the risk of throwing the engine off the line. But after a dozen pushes had been given with apparently little result a shell struck the front of the engine, setting fire to the woodwork, and he thereupon turned on more steam, and with considerable momentum we struck the obstacle once more. There was a grinding crash; the engine staggered, checked, shore forward again, until with a clanging, tearing sound it broke past the point of interception, and nothing but the smooth line lay between us and home.

Brilliant success now seemed won, for I thought that the rear and gun trucks were following the locomotive, and that all might squeeze into them, and so make an honourable escape. But the longed-for cup was dashed aside. Looking backward, I saw that the couplings had parted or had been severed by a shell, and that the trucks still lay on the wrong side of the obstruction, separated by it from the engine. No one dared to risk imprisoning the engine again by making it go back for the trucks, so an attempt was made to drag the trucks up to the engine. Owing chiefly to the fire of the enemy this failed completely, and Captain Haldane determined to be content with saving the locomotive. He accordingly permitted the driver to retire along the line slowly, so that the infantry might get as much shelter from the ironwork of the engine as possible, and the further idea was to get into some houses near the station, about 800 yards away, and there hold out while the engine went for assistance.

As many wounded as possible were piled

on to the engine, standing in the cab, lying on the tender, or clinging to the cowcatcher. And all this time the shells fell into the wet earth throwing up white clouds, burst with terrifying detonations overhead, or actually struck the engine and the iron wreckage. Besides the three field-guns,

which proved to be
15-pounders, the
shell-firing Maxim
continued its work,
and its little shells,
discharged with an
ugly thud, thud,
thud, exploded with
startling bangs
on all sides. One I
remember struck
the footplate of the
engine scarcely a
yard from my face,
lit up into a bright
yellow flash, and

left me wondering why I was still alive. Another hit the coals in the tender, hurling a black shower into the air. A third—this also I saw—struck the arm of a private in the Dublin Fusiliers. The whole arm was smashed to a horrid pulp—bones, muscle, blood, and uniform all mixed together. At the bottom hung the hand, unhurt, but swelled instantly to three times its ordinary size. The engine was soon crowded and began to steam homewards—a mournful, sorely battered locomotive—with the woodwork of the firebox in flames and the water spouting from its pierced tanks.

The infantrymen straggled along beside it at the double.

Seeing the engine escaping the Boers increased their fire, and the troops, hitherto somewhat protected by the iron trucks, began to suffer. The major of volunteers fell, shot through the thigh. Here and there men dropped on the ground, several screamed—this is very rare in war—and cried for help. About a quarter of the force was very soon killed or wounded. The shells which pursued the retreating soldiers scattered them all along the track. Order and control vanished. The engine, increasing its pace, drew out from the thin crowd of fugitives and was soon in safety. The infantry continued to run down the line in the direction of the houses, and, in spite of their disorder, I honestly consider that they were capable of making a further resistance when some shelter should be reached. But at this moment one of those miserable incidents—much too frequent in this war—occurred.

A private soldier who was wounded, in direct disobedience of the positive orders that no surrender was to be made, took it on himself to wave a pocket-handkerchief. The Boers immediately ceased firing, and with equal daring and humanity a dozen horsemen galloped from the hills into the scattered fugitives, scarcely any of whom had seen the white flag, and several of whom were still firing, and called loudly on them to surrender. Most of the soldiers, uncertain what to do, then halted, gave up their arms, and became prisoners of war. Those further away from the horsemen continued to run and were shot or hunted down in twos and threes, and some made good their escape.

For my part I found myself on the engine when the obstruction was at last passed and remained there jammed in the cab next to the man with the shattered arm. In this way I travelled some 500 yards, and passed through the fugitives, noticing particularly a young officer, Lieutenant Frankland, who with a happy, confident smile on his face was endeavouring to rally his men. When I approached the houses where we had resolved to make a stand, I jumped on to the line, in order to collect the men as they arrived, and hence the address from which this letter is written, for scarcely had the locomotive left me than I found myself alone in a shallow cutting and none of our soldiers, who had all surrendered on the way, to be seen. Then suddenly there appeared on the line at the end of the cutting two men not in uniform. 'Platelayers,' I said to myself, and then, with a surge of realisation, 'Boers.' My mind retains a momentary impression of these tall figures, full of animated movement, clad in dark flapping clothes, with slouch, storm-driven hats poising on their rifles hardly a hundred yards away. I turned and ran between the rails of the track, and the only thought I achieved was this, 'Boer marksmanship.' Two bullets passed, both within a foot, one on either side. I flung myself against the banks of the cutting. But they gave no cover. Another glance at the figures; one was now kneeling to aim. Again I darted forward. Movement seemed the only chance. Again two soft kisses sucked in the air, but nothing struck me. This could not endure. I must get out of the cutting—that damnable corridor. I scrambled up the bank. The earth sprang up beside me, and something touched my hand, but outside the cutting was a tiny depression. I crouched in this, struggling to get my wind. On the other side of the railway a horseman galloped up, shouting to me and waving his hand. He was scarcely forty yards off. With a rifle I could have killed him easily.

I knew nothing of white flags, and the bullets had made me savage. I reached down for my Mauser pistol. 'This one at least,' I said, and indeed it was a certainty; but alas! I had left the weapon in the cab of the engine in order to be free to work at the wreckage. What then? There was a wire fence between me and the horseman. Should I continue to fly? The idea of another shot at such a short range decided me. Death stood before me, grim sullen Death without his light-hearted companion, Chance. So I held up my hand, and like Mr. Jorrocks's foxes, cried 'Capivy.' Then I was herded with the other prisoners in a miserable group, and about the same time I noticed that my hand was bleeding, and it began to pour with rain.

Two days before I had written to an officer in high command at home, whose friendship I have the honour to enjoy: 'There has been a great deal too much surrendering in this war, and I hope people who do so will not be encouraged.' Fate had intervened, yet though her tone was full of irony she seemed to say, as I think Ruskin once said, 'It matters very little whether your judgments of people are true or untrue, and very much whether they are kind or unkind,' and repeating that I will make an end.

PRISONERS OF WAR

Pretoria: November
24, 1899.

The position of a
prisoner of war
is painful and
humiliating. A man
tries his best to kill
another, and finding
that he cannot
succeed asks his
enemy for mercy.

The laws of war demand that this should be accorded, but it is impossible not to feel a sense of humbling obligation to the captor from whose hand we take our lives. All military pride, all independence of spirit must be put aside. These may be carried to the grave, but not into captivity. We must prepare ourselves to submit, to obey, to endure. Certain things—sufficient food and water and protection during good behaviour—the victor must supply or be a savage, but beyond these all else is favour. Favours must be accepted from those with whom we have a long and bitter quarrel, from those who feel fiercely that we seek to do them cruel injustice. The dog who has been whipped must be thankful for the bone that is flung to him.

When the prisoners captured after the destruction of the armoured train had been disarmed and collected in a group we found that there were fifty-six unwounded or slightly wounded men, besides the more serious cases lying on the scene of the fight. The Boers crowded round, looking curiously at their prize, and we ate a little chocolate that by good fortune— for we had had no breakfast—was in our pockets, and sat down on the muddy ground to think. The rain streamed down from a dark leaden sky, and the coats of the horses steamed in the damp. 'Voorwärts,' said a voice, and, forming in a miserable procession, two wretched officers, a bare-headed, tattered Correspondent, four sailors with straw hats and

'H.M.S. Tartar' in gold letters on the ribbons—ill-timed jauntiness—some fifty soldiers and volunteers, and two or three railwaymen, we started, surrounded by the active Boer horsemen. Yet, as we climbed the low hills that surrounded the place of combat I looked back and saw the engine steaming swiftly away beyond Frere Station. Something at least was saved from the ruin; information would be carried to the troops at Estcourt, a good many of the troops and some of the wounded would escape, the locomotive was itself of value, and perhaps in saving all these things some little honour had been saved as well.

'You need not walk fast,' said a Boer in excellent English; 'take your time.' Then another, seeing me hatless in the downpour, threw me a soldier's cap—one of the Irish Fusilier caps, taken, probably, near Ladysmith. So they were not cruel men, these enemy. That was a great surprise to me, for I had read much of the literature of this land of lies, and fully expected every hardship and indignity. At length we reached the guns which had played on us for so many minutes— two strangely long barrels sitting very low on carriages of four wheels, like a break in which horses are exercised. They looked offensively modern, and I wondered why our Army had not got field artillery with fixed ammunition and 8,000 yards range. Some officers and men of the Staats Artillerie, dressed in a drab uniform with blue facings, approached us.

The commander, Adjutant Roos—as he introduced himself—made a polite salute. He regretted the unfortunate circumstances of our meeting; he complimented the officers on their defence—of course, it was hopeless from the first; he trusted his fire had not annoyed us; we should, he thought, understand the necessity for them to continue; above all he wanted to know how the engine had been able to get away, and how the line could have been cleared of wreckage under his guns. In fact, he behaved as a good professional soldier should, and his manner impressed me.

We waited here near the guns for half an hour, and meanwhile the Boers searched amid the wreckage for dead and wounded. A few of the wounded were brought to where we were, and laid on the ground, but most of them were placed in the shelter of one of the overturned trucks. As I write I do not know with any certainty what the total losses were, but the Boers say that they buried five dead, sent ten seriously wounded into Ladysmith, and kept three severely wounded in their field ambulances. Besides this, we are told that sixteen severely wounded escaped on the engine, and we have with the prisoners seven men, including myself, slightly wounded by splinters or injured in the derailment. If this be approximately correct, it seems that the casualties in the hour and a half of fighting were between thirty-five and forty: not many, perhaps, considering the fire, but out of 120 enough at least.

After a while we

were ordered to march on, and looking over the crest of the hill a strange and impressive sight met the eye. Only about 300 men had attacked the train, and I had thought that this was the enterprise of a separate detachment, but as the view extended I saw that this was

only a small part
of a large, powerful
force marching
south, under the
personal direction
of General Joubert,
to attack Estcourt.
Behind every hill,
thinly veiled by
the driving rain,
masses of mounted
men, arranged in
an orderly disorder,
were halted, and
from the rear long
columns of horsemen

rode steadily forward. Certainly I did not see less than 3,000, and I did not see nearly all. Evidently an important operation was in progress, and a collision either at Estcourt or Mooi River impended. This was the long expected advance: worse late than never.

Our captors conducted us to a rough tent which had been set up in a hollow in one of the hills, and which we concluded was General Joubert's headquarters. Here we were formed in a line, and soon surrounded by a bearded crowd of Boers cloaked in mackintosh. I explained that

I was a Special Correspondent, and asked to see General Joubert. But in the throng it was impossible to tell who were the superiors. My credentials were taken from me by a man who said he was a Field Cornet, and who promised that they should be laid before the General forthwith.

Meanwhile we waited in the rain, and the Boers questioned us. My certificate as a correspondent bore a name better known than liked in the Transvaal. Moreover, some of the private soldiers had been talking. 'You are the son of Lord Randolph Churchill?' said a Scottish Boer, abruptly. I did not deny the fact. Immediately there was much talking, and all crowded round me, looking and pointing, while I heard my name repeated on every side. 'I am a newspaper correspondent,' I said, 'and you ought not to hold me prisoner.' The Scottish Boer laughed. 'Oh,' he said, 'we do not catch lords' sons every day.' Whereat they all chuckled, and began to explain that I should be allowed to play football at Pretoria.

All this time I was expecting to be brought before General Joubert, from whom I had some hopes I should obtain assurances that my character as a press correspondent would be respected. But suddenly a mounted man rode up and ordered the prisoners to march away towards Colenso. The escort, twenty horsemen, closed round us. I addressed their leader, and demanded either that I should be taken before the General, or that my credentials should be given back. But the so-called Field Cornet was not to be seen. The only response was, 'Voorwärts,' and as it seemed useless, undignified, and even dangerous to discuss the matter further with these people, I turned and marched off with the rest.

We tramped for six hours across sloppy

fields and along tracks deep and slippery with mud, while the rain fell in a steady downpour and soaked everyone to the skin. The Boer escort told us several times not to hurry and to go our own pace, and once they allowed us to halt for a few moments. But we had had neither food nor water, and it was with a feeling of utter weariness that I saw the tin roofs of Colenso rise in the distance. We were put into a corrugated iron shed near the station, the floors of which were four inches deep with torn railway forms and account books. Here we flung ourselves down exhausted, and what with the shame, the disappointment, the excitement of the morning, the misery of the present, and physical weakness, it seemed that love of life was gone, and I thought almost with envy of a soldier I had seen during the fight lying quite still on the embankment, secure in the calm philosophy of death from 'the slings and arrows of outrageous fortune.'

After the Boers had lit two fires they opened one of the doors of the shed and told us we might come forth and dry ourselves. A newly slaughtered ox lay on the ground, and strips of his flesh were given to us. These we toasted on sticks over the fire and ate greedily, though since the animal had been alive five minutes before one felt a kind of cannibal. Other Boers not of our escort who were occupying Colenso came to look at us. With two of these who were brothers, English by race, Afrikanders by birth, Boers by choice, I had some conversation. The war, they said, was going well. Of course, it was a great matter to face the power and might of the British Empire, still they were resolved. They would drive the English out of South Africa for ever, or else fight to the last man. I said:

'You attempt the impossible. Pretoria will be taken by the middle of March.

What hope have you of withstanding a hundred thousand soldiers?'

'If I thought,' said the younger of the two brothers vehemently, 'that the Dutchmen would give in because Pretoria was taken, I would smash my rifle on those metals this very moment. We will fight for ever.' I could only reply:

'Wait and see how you feel when the tide is running the other way. It does not seem so easy to die when death is near.'

The man said, 'I will wait.'

Then we made friends. I told him that I hoped he would come safely through the war, and live to see a happier and a nobler South Africa under the flag which had been good enough for his forefathers; and he took off his blanket— which he was wearing with a hole in the middle like a cloak—and gave it to me to sleep in. So we parted, and presently, as night fell, the Field Cornet who had us in charge bade us carry a little forage into the shed to sleep on, and then locked us up in the dark, soldiers, sailors, officers, and Correspondent—a broken-spirited jumble.

I could not sleep. Vexation of spirit, a cold night, and wet clothes withheld sweet oblivion. The rights and wrongs of the quarrel, the fortunes and chances of the war, forced themselves on the mind. What men they were, these Boers! I thought of them as I had seen them in the morning riding forward through the rain—thousands of independent riflemen, thinking for themselves, possessed of beautiful weapons, led with skill, living as they rode without commissariat or transport or ammunition column, moving like the wind, and supported by iron constitutions and a stern, hard Old Testament God who should surely smite the Amalekites hip and thigh. And then, above the rain storm that beat loudly on the corrugated iron, I heard the sound of a chaunt. The Boers were singing their evening psalm, and the menacing notes—more full of indignant war than love and mercy—struck a chill into my heart, so that I thought after all that the war was unjust, that the Boers were better men than we, that Heaven was against us, that Ladysmith, Mafeking, and Kimberley would fall, that the Estcourt garrison would perish, that foreign Powers would intervene, that we should lose South Africa, and that would be the beginning of the end. So for the time I despaired of the Empire, nor was it till the morning sun—all the brighter after the rain storms, all

the warmer after
the chills—struck
in through the
windows that things
reassumed their
true colours and
proportions.

THROUGH THE
DUTCH CAMPS

Pretoria: November
30, 1899.

The bitter wind
of disappointment

pierces even the cloak of sleep. Moreover, the night was cold and the wet clothes chilled and stiffened my limbs, provoking restless and satisfactory dreams. I was breakfasting with President Kruger and General Joubert. 'Have some jam,' said the President. 'Thanks,' I replied, 'I would rather have marmalade.' But there was none. Their evident embarrassment communicated itself to me. 'Never mind,' I said, 'I'd just as soon have jam.' But the President was deeply moved. 'No, no,' he cried; 'we are not barbarians. Whatever you are entitled to you shall have, if I have to send to Johannesburg for it.'

So he got up to ring the bell, and with the clang I woke.

The first light of dawn was just peering in through the skylight of the corrugated iron shed. The soldiers lay in a brown litter about the floor, several snoring horribly. The meaning of it came home with a slap. Imprisoned; not able to come and go at will; about to be dragged off and put in some secluded place while others fought the great quarrel to the end; out of it all—like a pawn taken early in the game and flung aside into the box. I groaned with vexation, and, sitting up, aroused Frankland, who shared my blanket.

Then the Boers unlocked the doors and ordered us to get ready to march at once.

The forage which we had spread on the floor rustled, and the first idea of escape crossed my mind. Why not lie buried underneath this litter until prisoners and escort had marched away together? Would they count? Would they notice? I did not think so. They would reason—we know they all went in; it is certain none could have escaped during the night: therefore all must be here this morning. Suppose they missed me? 'Where is the "reporter," with whom we talked last evening?' Haldane would reply that he must have slipped out of the door before it was shut. They might scour the country; but would they search the shed? It seemed most unlikely. The scheme pleased my fancy exceedingly, and I was just resolving to conceal myself, when one of the guards entered and ordered everyone to file out forthwith.

We chewed a little more of the ox, slain and toasted the night before, and drank some rainwater from a large puddle, and, after this frugal breakfast, intimated that we were ready. Then we set out—a sorry gang of dirty, tramping prisoners, but yesterday the soldiers of the

Queen; while the fierce old farmers cantered their ponies about the veldt or closed around the column, looking at us from time to time with irritating disdain and still more irritating pity. We marched across the waggon bridge of the Tugela, and following the road, soon entered the hills. Among these we journeyed for several hours, wading across the gullies which the heavy rains had turned into considerable streams and persecuted by the slanting rays of the sun. Here and there parties of Boers met us, and much handshaking and patting on the back ensued between the newcomers and our escort. Once we halted at a little field hospital—a dozen tents and waggons with enormous red-cross flags, tucked away in a deep hollow.

We passed through Pieters without a check at the same toilsome plod and on to Nelthorpe. Here we began to approach the Dutch lines of investment round Ladysmith, and the advance of half an hour brought us to a very strong picket, where we were ordered to halt and rest. Nearly two hundred Boers swarmed round in a circle and began at once—for they are all keen politicians and as curious as children—to ask questions of every sort. What did we think of South Africa? Would we like to go in an armoured train again? How long would the English go on fighting? When would the war end? and the reply, 'When you are beaten,' was received with shouts of laughter.

'Oh no, old chappie, you can never beat us. Look at Mafeking. We have taken

Mafeking. You will find Baden Powell waiting for you at Pretoria. Kimberley, too, will fall this week. Rhodes is trying to escape in a balloon, disguised as a woman—a fine woman.' Great merriment at this. 'What about Ladysmith?' 'Ten days. Ten days more and then we shall have some whisky.'

Listen. There was the boom of a heavy gun, and, turning, I saw the white cloud of smoke hanging on the crest of Bulwana.

'That goes on always,' said the Boer. 'Can any soldiers bear that long? Oh, you will find all the English army at Pretoria. Indeed, if it were not for the sea-sickness we would take England. Besides, do you think the European Powers will allow you to bully us?'

I said, 'Why bully if you are so strong?'

'Well, why should you come and invade our country?'

'Your country? I thought this was Natal.'

'So it is: but Natal is ours. You stole it from us. Now we take it back again. That's all.'

A hum of approval ran round the grinning circle. An old Boer came up. He did not understand what induced the soldiers to go in the armoured train. Frankland replied, 'Ordered to. Don't

you have to obey
your orders?'

The old man
shook his head in
bewilderment, then
he observed, 'I fight
to kill: I do not fight
to be killed. If the
Field Cornet was to
order me to go in
an armoured train,
I would say to him,
"Field Cornet, go to
hell."'

'Ah, you are not

soldiers.'

'But we catch soldiers and kill soldiers and make soldiers run away.'

There was a general chorus of 'Yaw, yaw, yaw,' and grunts of amusement.

'You English,' said a well-dressed man, 'die for your country: we Afrikanders live for ours.'

I said, 'Surely you don't think you will win this war?'

'Oh, yes; we will win all right this time, just the same as before.'

'But it is not the same as before. Gladstone is dead, they are determined at home. If necessary they will send three hundred thousand men and spend a hundred millions.'

'We are not afraid; no matter how many thousand penny soldiers you send,' and an English Boer added, 'Let 'em all come.'

But there was one discordant note in the full chorus of confidence. It recurred again and again. 'Where is Buller?' 'When is

Buller coming?'
These merry fellows
were not without
their doubts.

'He will come when
the army is ready.'

'But we have beaten
the army.'

'No, the war has not
begun yet.'

'It's all over for you,
old chappie, anyway.'

It was a fair hit. I

joined the general laughter, and, reviewing the incident by the light of subsequent events, feel I had some right to.

Very soon after this we were ordered to march again, and we began to move to the eastward in the direction of the Bulwana Hill, descending as we did so into the valley of the Klip River. The report of the intermittent guns engaged in the bombardment of Ladysmith seemed very loud and near, and the sound of the British artillery making occasional reply could be plainly distinguished. After we had crossed the railway line beyond Nelthorpe I caught sight of another evidence of the proximity of friends. High above the hills, to the left of the path, hung a speck of gold-beater's skin. It was the Ladysmith balloon. There, scarcely two miles away, were safety and honour. The soldiers noticed the balloon too. 'Those are our blokes,' they said. 'We ain't all finished yet,' and so they comforted themselves, and a young sergeant advanced a theory that the garrison would send out cavalry to rescue us.

We kept our eyes on the balloon till it was hidden by the hills, and I thought of all that lay at the bottom of its rope. Beleaguered

Ladysmith, with its shells, its flies, its fever, and its filth seemed a glorious paradise to me.

We forded the Klip River breast high, and, still surrounded by our escort, trudged on towards the laagers behind Bulwana. But it was just three o'clock, after about ten hours' marching, that

we reached the camp
where we were to
remain for the night.
Having had no food—
except the toasted
ox, a disgusting form
of nourishment—
and being besides
unused to walking
far, I was so utterly
worn out on arrival
that at first I cared
for nothing but
to lie down under
the shade of a
bush. But after the

Field-Cornet had given us some tea and bully beef, and courteously bidden us to share the shelter of his tent, I felt equal to further argument.

The Boers were delighted and crowded into the small tent.

'Will you tell us why there is this war?'

I said that it was because they wanted to beat us out of South Africa and we did not like the idea.

'Oh no, that is not the reason.' Now that the war had begun they would drive the British into the sea; but if we had been content with what we had they would not have interfered with us—except to get a port and have their full independence recognised.

'I will tell you what is the real cause of this war. It's all those damned capitalists. They want to steal our country, and they have bought Chamberlain, and now these three, Rhodes, Beit, and Chamberlain, think they will have the

Rand to divide between them afterwards.'

'Don't you know that the gold mines are the property of the shareholders, many of whom are foreigners—Frenchman and Germans and others? After the war, whatever government rules, they will still belong to these people.'

'What are we fighting for then?'

'Because you hate us bitterly, and have armed yourselves in order to attack us, and we naturally chose to fight when we are not occupied elsewhere. "Agree with thine adversary whiles thou art in the way with him."'"

'Don't you think it wicked to try to steal our country?'

'We only want to protect ourselves and our own interests. We didn't want your country.'

'No, but the damned capitalists do.'

'If you had tried to keep on friendly terms with us there would have been no war. But you want to drive us out of South Africa. Think of a great Afrikander Republic—all South Africa speaking Dutch—a United States under your President and your Flag, sovereign and international.'

Their eyes glittered. 'That's what we want,' said one. 'Yaw, yaw,' said the others, 'and that's what we're going to have.'

'Well, that's the reason of the war.'

'No, no. You know it's those damned capitalists and Jews who have caused the war.' And the argument recommenced its orbit.

So the afternoon wore away.

As the evening fell the Commandant required us to withdraw to some tents which had been pitched at the corner of the laager. A special tent was provided for the officers, and now, for the first time, they found themselves separated from their men. I had a moment in which to decide whether I would rank as officer or private, and chose the former, a choice I was soon to regret. Gradually it became night. The scene as the daylight faded was striking and the circumstances were impressive. The dark shadow of Bulwana mountain flung back over the Dutch camp, and the rugged, rock-strewn hills rose about it on all sides.

The great waggons were arranged to enclose a square, in the midst of which stood clusters of variously shaped tents and lines of munching oxen. Within the laager and around it little fires began to glow, and by their light the figures of the Boers could be seen busy cooking and eating their suppers, or smoking in moody, muttering groups. All was framed by the triangular doorway of the tent, in which two ragged, bearded men sat nursing their rifles and gazing at their captives in silence. Nor was it till my companions prepared to sleep that the stolid guards summoned the energy and wit to ask, in struggling

English (for these were real veldt Boers), the inevitable question, 'And after all, what are we fighting for? Why is there this war?' But I was tired of arguing, so I said, 'It is the will of God,' and turned to rest with a more confident feeling than the night before, for I felt that these men were wearying of the struggle.

To rest but not
to sleep, for the
knowledge that
the British lines at
Ladysmith lay only
five miles away filled
my brain with hopes
and plans of escape.
I had heard it said
that all Dutchmen
slept between 12
and 2 o'clock, and
I waited, trusting
that our sentries

would observe the national custom. But I soon saw that I should have been better situated with the soldiers. We three officers were twenty yards from the laager, and around our little tent, as I learned by peering through a rent in the canvas, no less than four men were posted. At intervals they were visited or relieved, at times they chatted together; but never for a minute was their vigilance relaxed, and the continual clicking of the Mauser breech bolts, as they played with their rifles, unpleasantly proclaimed their attention. The moon was full and bright, and it was obvious that no possible chance of success awaited an attempt.

With the soldiers the circumstances were more favourable. Their tent stood against the angle of the laager, and although the sentries watched the front and sides it seemed to me that a man might crawl through the back, and by walking boldly across the laager itself pass safely out into the night. It was certainly a road none would expect a fugitive to take; but whatever its chances it was closed to me, for the guard was changed at midnight and a new sentry stationed between our tent and those near the laager.

I examined him

through the torn tent. He was quite a child—a boy of about fourteen—and needless to say appreciated the importance of his duties. He played this terrible game of soldiers with all his heart and soul; so at last I abandoned the idea of flight and fell asleep.

In the morning,

before the sun was up, the Commandant Davel came to rouse us. The prisoners were to march at once to Elandslaagte Station. 'How far?' we asked, anxiously, for all were very footsore. 'Only a very little way—five hours' slow walking.' We stood up—for we had slept in our clothes and cared nothing for washing—and said that we were ready. The Commandant then departed, to return in a few minutes bringing some tea and bully beef, which he presented to us with an apology for the plainness of the fare. He asked an English-speaking Boer to explain that they had nothing better themselves. After we had eaten and were about to set forth, Dayel said, through his interpreter, that he would like to know from us that we were satisfied with the treatment we met with at his laager. We gladly gave him the assurance, and with much respect bade good-bye to this dignified and honourable enemy. Then we were marched away over the hills towards the north, skirting the picket line round Ladysmith to the left. Every half-mile or so the road led through or by some Boer laager, and the occupants—for it was a quiet day in the batteries—turned out in hundreds to look at us. I do not know how many men I saw, but certainly during this one march not less than 5,000. Of this great number two only offered insults to the gang of prisoners. One was a dirty, mean-looking little Hollander. He said, 'Well, Tommy, you've got your franchise, anyhow.' The other was an Irishman. He addressed himself to Frankland, whose badges proclaimed

his regiment.
What he said when
disentangled from
obscenity amounted
to this: 'I am glad
to see you Dublin
fellows in trouble.'
The Boers silenced
him at once and we
passed on. But that
was all the taunting
we received during
the whole journey
from Frere Station
to Pretoria, and
when one remembers

that the Burghers are only common men with hardly any real discipline, the fact seems very remarkable. But little and petty as it was it galled horribly. The soldiers felt the sting and scowled back; the officers looked straight before them. Yet it was a valuable lesson. Only a few days before I had read in the newspapers of how the Kaffirs had jeered at the Boer prisoners when they were marched into Pietermaritzburg, saying, 'Where are your passes?' It had seemed a very harmless joke then, but now I understood how a prisoner feels these things.

It was about eleven o'clock

when we reached Elandslaagte Station. A train awaited the prisoners. There were six or seven closed vans for the men and a first-class carriage for the officers. Into a compartment of this we were speedily bundled. Two Boers with rifles sat themselves between us, and the doors were locked. I was desperately hungry, and asked for both food and water. 'Plenty is coming,' they said, so we waited patiently, and sure enough, in a few minutes a railway official came along the platform, opened the door, and thrust before us in generous profusion two tins of preserved mutton, two tins of preserved fish, four or five loaves, half a dozen pots of jam, and a large can of tea. As far as I could see the soldiers fared no worse. The reader will believe that we did not stand on ceremony, but fell to at once and made the first satisfying meal for three days. While we ate a great crowd of Boers gathered around the train and peered curiously in at the windows. One of them was a doctor, who, noticing that my hand was bound up, inquired whether I were wounded. The cut caused by the splinter of bullet was insignificant, but since it was ragged and had received no attention for two days it had begun to fester. I therefore showed him my hand, and he immediately bustled off to get bandages and hot water and what not, with which, amid the approving grins of the rough fellows who thronged the platform, he soon bound me up very correctly.

The train whereby we were to travel was required for other business besides; and I noticed about a hundred Boers embarking with their horses in a dozen large cattle trucks behind the engine. At or about noon we steamed off, moving slowly along the line, and Captain Haldane pointed out to me the ridge of Elandslaagte, and gave me some further account of that successful action and of the great skill with which Hamilton had directed the infantry attack. The two Boers who were guarding us listened with great interest, but the single observation they made was that we had only to fight Germans and Hollanders at Elandslaagte. 'If these had been veldt Boers in front of you——' My companion replied that even then the Gordon Highlanders might have made some progress. Whereat both Boers laughed softly and shook their heads with the air of a wiseacre, saying, 'You will know better when you're as old as me,' a remark I constantly endure from very worthy people.

Two stations beyond
Elandslaagte the
Boer commando,
or portion of
commando, left the
train, and the care
and thought that
had been lavished
on the military
arrangements
were very evident.
All the stations
on the line were
fitted with special
platforms three or
four hundred yards

long, consisting of earth embankments revetted with wood towards the line and sloping to the ground on the other side. The horsemen were thereby enabled to ride their horses out of the trucks, and in a few minutes all were cantering away across the plain. One of the Boer guards noticed the attention I paid to these arrangements. 'It is in case we have to go back quickly to the Biggarsberg or Laing's Nek,' he explained. As we travelled on I gradually fell into conversation with this man. His name, he told me, was Spaarwater, which he pronounced Spare-water. He was a farmer from the Ermolo district.

In times of peace
he paid little or no
taxes. For the last
four years he had
escaped altogether.
The Field Cornet,
he remarked, was
a friend of his. But
for such advantages
he lay under the
obligation to serve
without pay in
war-time, providing
horse, forage,
and provisions.
He was a polite,

meek-mannered little man, very anxious in all the discussion to say nothing that could hurt the feelings of his prisoners, and I took a great liking to him. He had fought at Dundee. 'That,' he said, 'was a terrible battle. Your artillery? Bang! bang! bang! came the shells all round us. And the bullets! Whew, don't tell me the soldiers can't shoot. They shoot jolly well, old chappie. I, too, can shoot. I can hit a bottle six times out of seven at a hundred yards, but when there is a battle then I do not shoot so well.'

The other man, who understood a little English, grinned at this, and muttered something in Dutch.

'What does he say?' I inquired.

'He says "He too,"' replied Spaarwater. 'Besides, we cannot see your soldiers. At Dundee I was looking down the hill and saw nothing except rows of black boots marching and the black belts of one of the regiments.'

'But,' I said, 'you managed to hit some of them after all.'

He smiled, 'Ah, yes, we are lucky, and God is on our side. Why, after Dundee, when we were retiring, we had to cross a great open plain, never even an ant-hill, and you had put twelve great cannons—I counted them—and Maxims as well, to shoot us as we went; but not one fired a shot. Was it not God's hand that stopped them? After that we knew.'

I said: 'Of course the guns did not fire, because you had raised the white flag.'

'Yes,' he answered, 'to ask for armistice, but not to give in. We are not going to give in yet. Besides, we have heard that your Lancers speared our wounded at Elandslaagte.' We were getting on dangerous ground. He hastened to turn the subject. 'It's all those lying newspapers that spread these reports on both sides, just like the capitalists made the war by lying.'

A little further on

the ticket collector came to join in the conversation. He was a Hollander, and very eloquent.

'Why should you English take this country away from us?' he asked, and the silent Boer chimed in broken English. 'Are not our farms our own? Why must we fight for them?'

I endeavoured to explain the ground of our quarrel. 'After all British government is not a tyranny.'

'It's no good for a working-man,' said the ticket collector; 'look at Kimberley. Kimberley was a good place to live in before the capitalists collared it. Look at it now. Look at me. What are my wages?'

I forget what he said they were, but they were extraordinary wages for a ticket collector.

'Do you suppose I should get such wages under the English Government?'

I said 'No.'

'There you are,' he said. 'No English Government for me,' and added

inconsequently,
'We fight for our freedom.'

Now I thought I had an argument that would tell. I turned th the farmer, who had been listening approvingly:

'Those are very good wages.'

'Ah, yes.'

'Where does the

money come from?'

'Oh, from the taxes ... and from the railroad.'

'Well, now, you send a good deal of your produce by rail, I suppose?'

'Ya' (an occasional lapse into Dutch).

'Don't you find the rates very high?'

'Ya, ya,' said both

the Boers together;
'very high.'

'That is because
he' (pointing to the
ticket collector)
'is getting such
good wages. You
are paying them.'
At this they both
laughed heartily, and
Spaarwater said that
that was quite true,
and that the rates
were too high.

'Under the English

Government,' I said, 'he will not get such high wages; you will not have to pay such high rates.'

They received the conclusion in silence. Then Spaarwater said, 'Yes, but we shall have to pay a tribute to your Queen.'

'Does Cape Colony?' I asked.

'Well, what about that ironclad?'

'A present, a free-will offering because they are contented—as you will be some day—under our flag.'

'No, no, old chappie, we don't want your flag; we want to be left alone. We are free, you are not free.'

'How do you mean

"not free"?'

'Well, is it right that a dirty Kaffir should walk on the pavement—without a pass too? That's what they do in your British Colonies. Brother! Equal! Ugh! Free! Not a bit. We know how to treat Kaffirs.'

Probing at random I had touched a very sensitive nerve.

We had got down
from underneath
the political and
reached the social.
What is the true
and original root
of Dutch aversion
to British rule? It is
not Slagters Nek,
nor Broomplatz,
nor Majuba, nor
the Jameson Raid.
Those incidents only
fostered its growth.
It is the abiding
fear and hatred of

the movement that
seeks to place the
native on a level
with the white man.
British government
is associated in the
Boer farmer's mind
with violent social
revolution. Black is
to be proclaimed
the same as white.
The servant is to be
raised against the
master; the Kaffir
is to be declared
the brother of the

European, to be constituted his legal equal, to be armed with political rights. The dominant race is to be deprived of their superiority; nor is a tigress robbed of her cubs more furious than is the Boer at this prospect.

I mused on the tangled skein of politics and party principles. This Boer farmer was a very typical character, and represented to my mind all that was best and noblest in the African Dutch character. Supposing he had been conducting Mr. Morley to Pretoria, not as a prisoner of war, but as an honoured guest, instead of me, what would their conversation have been? How excellently they would have agreed on the general question of the war! I could imagine the farmer purring with delight as his distinguished charge dilated in polished sentences upon liberty and the rights of nationalities. Both would together have bewailed the horrors of war and the crime of aggression;

both would have condemned the tendencies of modern Imperialism and Capitalism; both would have been in complete accord whenever the names of Rhodes, Chamberlain, or Milner were mentioned. And the spectacle of this citizen soldier, called reluctant, yet not unwilling, from the

quiet life of his farm
to fight bravely in
defence of the soil
on which he lived,
which his fathers had
won by all manner of
suffering and peril,
and to preserve
the independence
which was his pride
and joy, against
great enemies of
regulars—surely that
would have drawn
the most earnest
sympathy of the

eminent idealist. And then suddenly a change, a jarring note in the duet of agreement.

'We know how to treat Kaffirs in this country. Fancy letting the black filth walk on the pavement!'

And after that no more agreement: but argument growing keener and keener; gulf widening every moment.

'Educate a Kaffir! Ah, that's you English all over. No, no, old chappie. We educate 'em with a stick. Treat 'em with humanity and consideration—I like that. They were put here by the God Almighty to work for us. We'll stand no damned nonsense from them. We'll keep them in their proper places. What do you think? Insist on their proper treatment will you? Ah, that's what we're going to see about now. We'll settle whether you English are to interfere with us before this war is over.'

The afternoon dragged away before the train passed near

Dundee. Lieutenant Frankland had helped to storm Talana Hill, and was much excited to see the field of battle again under these new circumstances. 'It would all have been different if Symons had lived. We should never have let them escape from under our guns. That commando would have been smashed up altogether.'

'But what about the other commando that came up the next day?'

'Oh, the General would have managed them all right. He'd have, soon found some way of turning them out.' Nor do I doubt he would, if the fearless confidence with which he inspired his troops could have protected his life. But the bullet is brutally indiscriminating, and before it the brain of a hero or the quarters of a horse stand exactly the same chance to the vertical square inch.

After Talana Hill was lost to view we began to search for Majuba, and saw it just as night closed in—a great dark mountain with memories as sad and gloomy as its appearance. The Boer guards pointed out to us where they had mounted their big cannons to defend Laing's Nek, and remarked that the pass was now impregnable. I could not resist saying, 'This is not the only road into the

Transvaal.' 'Ah, but you English always come where we want you to come.'

We now approached the frontier. I had indulged in hopes of leaving the train while in the Volksrust Tunnel by climbing out of the window. The possibility had, however, presented itself to Spaarwater, for he shut both windows, and just before we reached the entrance opened the breech of his Mauser to show me that it was fully loaded. So prudence again imposed patience. It was quite dark when the train reached Volksrust, and we knew ourselves actually in the enemy's country. The platform was densely crowded with armed Boers. It appeared that two new commandos had been called out, and were waiting for trains to take them to the front. Moreover, a strong raiding party had just come back from British Swaziland. The windows were soon blocked with the bearded faces of men who gazed stolidly and commented freely to each other on our appearance. It was like being a wild beast in a cage. After some time a young woman pushed her way to the window and had a prolonged stare, at the end of which she observed in a loud voice (I must record it)—'Why, they're not so bad looking after all.' At this there was general laughter, and Spaarwater, who was much concerned, said that they meant no harm, and that if we were annoyed he would have everyone cleared away. But I said: 'Certainly not; let them feast their eyes.' So they did, for forty minutes by the clock.

Their faces were plain and rough, but not unkindly. The

little narrow-set pig-eyes were the most displeasing feature. For the rest they looked what they were, honest ignorant peasants with wits sharpened by military training and the conditions of a new country. Presently I noticed at the window furthest from the platform one of quite a different type. A handsome boyish face without beard or moustache, and a very amiable expression. We looked at each other. There was no one else at that side of the carriage.

'Will you have some cigarettes?' he said, holding me out a packet. I took one, and we began to talk. 'Is there going to be much more war?' he inquired anxiously.

'Yes, very much more; we have scarcely begun,' He looked quite miserable.

I said, 'You have not been at the front yet?'

'No, I am only just commandeered.'

'How old are you?'

'Sixteen.'

'That's very young to go and fight.'

He shook his head sadly.

'What's your name?'

'Cameron.'

'That's not a Dutch name?'

'No, I'm not a Dutchman. My father came from Scotland.'

'Then why do you go and fight against the British?'

'How can I help it? I live here. You must go when you're commandeered. They wouldn't let me off. Mother tried her best. But it's "come out and fight or leave the country" here, and we've got nothing but the farm.'

'The Government would have paid you compensation afterwards.'

'Ah! that's what they told father last time. He was loyal, and helped to defend the Pretoria laager. He lost everything, and he had to begin all over again.'

'So now you fight against your country?'

'I can't help it,' he repeated sullenly, 'you must go when you're commandeered.' And then he climbed down off the footboard, and I did not see him again—one piteous item of Gladstone's legacy—the ruined and abandoned loyalist in the second generation.

Before the train

left Volksrust we
changed our guards.
The honest burghers
who had captured us
had to return to the
front, and we were
to be handed over to
the police. The leader
of the escort—a dear
old gentleman—I
am ignorant of
his official rank—
approached and
explained through
Spaarwater that
it was he who had

placed the stone and so caused our misfortunes. He said he hoped we bore no malice. We replied by no means, and that we would do the same for him with pleasure any day. Frankland asked him what rewards he would get for such distinguished service. In truth he might easily have been shot, had we turned the corner a minute earlier. The subaltern apparently contemplated some Republican V.C. or D.S.O. But the farmer was much puzzled by his question. After some explaining we learnt that he had been given fourteen days' furlough to go home to his farm and see his wife. His evident joy and delight were touching. I said 'Surely this is a very critical time to leave the front. You may miss an important battle.'

'Yes,' he replied simply, 'I hope so.' Then we said 'good-bye,' and I gave him, and also Spaarwater, a little slip of paper setting forth that they had shown kindness and courtesy to British prisoners of war, and personally requesting anyone into whose hands the papers might come to treat them well, should they themselves be taken by the Imperial forces.

We were then handed to a rather dilapidated policeman of a gendarme type, who spat copiously on the floor of the carriage and informed us that we should be shot if we attempted to escape. Having no desire to speak to this fellow, we let down the sleeping shelves of the compartment and, as the train steamed out of Volksrust, turned to sleep.

IN AFRIKANDER BONDS

Pretoria: December 3rd, 1899.

It was, as nearly as I can remember, midday when the train-load of prisoners reached Pretoria. We pulled up in a sort of siding with an earth platform on the right side which opened into the streets of the town. The day was fine, and the sun shone brightly. There was a considerable crowd of people to receive us; ugly women with bright parasols, loafers and ragamuffins, fat burghers too heavy to ride at the front, and a long line of untidy, white-helmeted policemen—'zarps' as they were called—who looked like broken-down constabulary. Someone opened—unlocked, that is, the point—the door of the railway carriage and told us to come out; and out we came—a very ragged and tattered group of officers—and waited under the sun blaze and the gloating of many eyes. About a dozen cameras were clicking busily, establishing an imperishable record of our shame. Then they loosed the men and bade them form in rank. The soldiers came out of the dark vans, in which they had been confined, with some eagerness, and began at once to chirp and joke, which seemed to me most ill-timed good humour. We waited altogether for about twenty minutes. Now for the first time since my capture I hated the enemy. The simple, valiant burghers at the front, fighting bravely as they had been told 'for their farms,' claimed respect, if not sympathy. But here in Pretoria all was petty and contemptible. Slimy, sleek officials

of all nationalities—
the red-faced,
snub-nosed Hollander,
the oily Portuguese
half-caste—thrust
or wormed their way
through the crowd
to look. I seemed to
smell corruption in
the air. Here were
the creatures who
had fattened on
the spoils. There in
the field were the
heroes who won
them. Tammany Hall

was defended by the Ironsides.

From these reflections I was recalled by a hand on my shoulder. A lanky, unshaven police sergeant grasped my arm. 'You are not an officer,' he said; 'you go this way with the common soldiers,' and he led me across the open space to where the men were formed in a column of fours. The crowd grinned: the cameras clicked again. I fell in with the soldiers and seized the opportunity to tell them not to laugh or smile, but to appear serious men who cared for the cause they fought for; and when I saw how readily they took the hint, and what influence I possessed with them, it seemed to me that perhaps with two thousand prisoners something some day might be done. But presently a superior official— superior in rank alone, for in other respects he looked a miserable creature— came up and led me back to the officers. At last, when the crowd had thoroughly satisfied their patriotic curiosity, we were marched off; the soldiers to the enclosed camp on the racecourse, the officers to the States Model Schools prison.

The distance was short, so far as we were concerned, and surrounded by an escort of three armed policemen to each officer, we swiftly traversed two sandy avenues with detached houses on either hand, and reached our destination. We turned a corner; on the other side of the road stood a long, low, red brick building with a slated verandah and a row of iron railings before it. The verandah was crowded with bearded men in khaki uniforms or brown suits of flannel—smoking, reading, or talking. They looked up as we arrived. The iron gate was opened, and passing in we joined sixty British officers 'held by the enemy;' and the iron gate was then shut again.

'Hullo! How are you? Where did they catch you? What's the latest news of

Buller's advance? Are we going to be exchanged?' and a dozen other questions were asked. It was the sort of reception accorded to a new boy at a private school, or, as it seemed to me, to a new arrival in hell. But after we had satisfied our friends in as much as we could, suggestions of baths, clothes, and luncheon were made which were very welcome. So we settled down to what promised to be a long and weary waiting.

The States Model Schools is a one-storied building of considerable size and solid structure, which occupies a corner formed by two roads through

Pretoria. It consists of twelve large class-rooms, seven or eight of which were used by the British officers as dormitories and one as a dining-room; a large lecture-hall, which served as an improvised fives-court; and a well-fitted gymnasium. It stood in a quadrangular playground about one hundred and twenty yards square, in which were a dozen tents for the police guards, a cookhouse, two tents for the soldier servants, and a newly set-up bath-shed. I do not know how the arrival of other prisoners may have modified these arrangements, but at the time of my coming into the prison, there was room enough for everyone.

The Transvaal Government provided a daily ration of bully beef and groceries, and the prisoners were allowed to purchase from the local storekeeper, a Mr. Boshof, practically everything they cared to order, except alcoholic liquors. During the first week of

my detention we
requested that
this last prohibition
might be withdrawn,
and after profound
reflection and much
doubtings, the
President consented
to countenance the
buying of bottled
beer. Until this
concession was
obtained our liquid
refreshment would
have satisfied the
most immoderate

advocate of temperance, and the only relief was found when the Secretary of State for War, a kind-hearted Portuguese, would smuggle in a bottle of whiskey hidden in his tail-coat pocket or amid a basket of fruit.

A very energetic and clever young officer of the Dublin Fusiliers, Lieutenant

Grimshaw, undertook the task of managing the mess, and when he was assisted by another subaltern— Lieutenant Southey, of the Royal Irish Fusiliers— this became an exceedingly well-conducted concern. In spite of the high prices prevailing in Pretoria—prices which were certainly not lowered for our benefit—the somewhat meagre rations which the Government allowed were supplemented, until we lived, for three shillings a day, quite as well as any regiment on service.

On arrival, every officer was given a new suit of clothes, bedding, towels, and toilet necessaries, and the indispensable

Mr, Boshof was prepared to add to this wardrobe whatever might be required on payment either in money or by a cheque on Messrs. Cox & Co., whose accommodating fame had spread even to this distant hostile town. I took an early opportunity to buy a suit of tweeds of a dark neutral colour, and as unlike the suits of clothes issued by the Government as possible. I would also have purchased a hat, but another officer told me that he had asked for one and had been refused. After all, what use could I find for a hat, when there were plenty of helmets to spare if I wanted to Walk in the courtyard? And yet my taste ran towards a slouch hat.

The case of the soldiers was less comfortable than ours. Their rations were very scanty: only one pound of bully beef once a week and two pounds of bread; the rest was made up with mealies, potatoes, and such-like—and not very much of them. Moreover, since they had no money of their own, and since prisoners of war received no pay, they were unable to buy even so much as a pound of tobacco. In consequence they complained a good deal, and were, I think, sufficiently discontented to require nothing but leading to make them rise against their guards.

The custody and regulating of the officers were entrusted to a board of management, four of whose members visited us frequently and listened to any complaints or requests. M. de Souza, the Secretary of War, was perhaps the most friendly and obliging of these, and I think we owed most of the indulgences to his representations. He was a far-seeing little man who had travelled to Europe, and had a very clear conception of the relative strengths of Britain and the Transvaal. He enjoyed a lucrative and influential position under the Government, and was therefore devoted to its interests, but he was nevertheless suspected by the Inner Ring of Hollanders and the Relations of the President of having some sympathy for the British. He had therefore to be very careful. Commandant Opperman, who was directly responsible for our safe custody, was in times of peace a Landrost or Justice. He was too fat to go and fight, but he was an honest and patriotic Boer, who would have gladly taken an active part in the war. He firmly believed that the Republics would win, and when, as sometimes happened, bad news reached Pretoria, Opperman looked a picture of misery, and would come to us and speak of his resolve to shoot his wife and children and perish in the defence of the capital. Dr. Gunning was an amiable little Hollander, fat, rubicund, and well educated. He was a keen politician, and much attached to the Boer Government, which paid him an excellent salary for looking after

the State Museum.
He had a wonderful
collection of postage
stamps, and was also
engaged in forming
a Zoological Garden.
This last ambition
had just before the
war led him into
most serious trouble,
for he was unable
to resist the lion
which Mr. Rhodes
had offered him.
He confided to me
that the President

had spoken 'most harshly' to him in consequence, and had peremptorily ordered the immediate return of the beast under threats of instant dismissal. Gunning said that he could not have borne such treatment, but that after all a man must live. My private impression is that he will acquiesce in any political settlement which leaves him to enlarge his museum undisturbed. But whether the Transvaal will be able to indulge in such luxuries, after blowing up many of other people's railway bridges, is a question which I cannot answer.

The fourth member of the Board, Mr.

Malan, was a foul and objectionable brute. His personal courage was better suited to insulting the prisoners in Pretoria than to fighting the enemy at the front. He was closely related to the President, but not even this advantage could altogether protect him from taunts of cowardice, which were made even in the Executive Council, and somehow filtered down to us. On one occasion he favoured me with some of his impertinence; but I reminded him that in war either side may win, and asked whether he was wise to place himself in a separate category as regards behaviour to the prisoners. 'Because,' quoth I, 'it might be so convenient to the British Government to be able to make one or two examples.' He was a great gross man, and his colour came and went on a large over-fed face; so that his uneasiness was obvious. He never came near me again, but some days later the news of a Boer success arrived,

and on the strength
of this he came
to the prison and
abused a subaltern in
the Dublin Fusiliers,
telling him that he
was no gentleman,
and other things
which it is not right
to say to a prisoner.
The subaltern
happens to be
exceedingly handy
with his fists, so that
after the war is over
Mr. Malan is going to

get his head punched quite independently of the general settlement.

Although, as I have frequently stated, there were no legitimate grounds of complaint against the treatment of British regular officers while prisoners of war, the days I passed at Pretoria were the most monotonous and among the most miserable of my life. Early in the sultry mornings, for the heat at this season of the year was great, the soldier servants—prisoners like ourselves—would bring us a cup of coffee, and sitting up in bed we began to smoke the cigarettes and cigars of another idle, aimless day. Breakfast was at nine: a nasty uncomfortable meal. The room was stuffy, and there are more enlivening spectacles than seventy British officers caught by Dutch farmers and penned together in confinement. Then came the long morning, to be killed somehow by reading, chess, or cards—and perpetual cigarettes. Luncheon at one: the same as breakfast, only more so; and then a longer afternoon to follow a long morning. Often some of the officers used to play rounders in the small yard which we had for exercise. But the rest walked moodily up and down, or lounged over the railings and returned the stares of the occasional passers-by. Later would come the 'Volksstem'— permitted by special indulgence—with its budget of lies.

Sometimes we get a little fillip of excitement. One evening, as I was leaning over the railings, more than forty yards from the nearest sentry, a short man with a red moustache walked quickly down the street, followed by two colley dogs. As he passed, but without altering his pace in the slightest, or even looking towards me, he said quite distinctly 'Methuen beat the Boers to hell at Belmont.' That night the air seemed cooler and the courtyard larger. Already we imagined the

Republics collapsing
and the bayonets of
the Queen's Guards
in the streets of
Pretoria. Next day
I talked to the War
Secretary. I had
made a large map
upon the wall and
followed the course
of the war as far as
possible by making
squares of red and
green paper to
represent the various
columns. I said: 'What

about Methuen? He has beaten you at Belmont. Now he should be across the Modder. In a few days he will relieve Kimberley.' De Souza shrugged his shoulders. 'Who can tell?' he replied; 'but,' he put his finger on the map, 'there stands old Piet Cronje in a position called Scholz Nek, and we don't think

Methuen will ever get past him.' The event justified his words, and the battle which we call Magersfontein (and ought to call 'Maasfontayne') the Boers call Scholz Nek.

Long, dull, and profitless were the days. I could not write, for the ink seemed to dry upon the pen. I could not read with any perseverance, and during the whole month I was locked up, I only completed Carlyle's 'History of Frederick the Great' and Mill's 'Essay on Liberty,' neither of which satisfied my peevish expectations. When at last the sun sank behind the fort upon the hill and twilight marked the end of another wretched day, I used to walk up and down the courtyard looking reflectively at the dirty, unkempt 'zarps' who stood on guard, racking my brains to find some way, by force or fraud, by steel or gold, of regaining my freedom. Little did these Transvaal Policemen think, as they leaned on their rifles, smoking and watching the 'tame officers,' of the dark schemes of which they were the object, or of the peril in which they would stand but for the difficulties that lay beyond the wall. For we would have made short work of them and their weapons any misty night could we but have seen our way clear after that.

As the darkness thickened, the electric lamps were switched on and the whole courtyard turned blue-white with black velvet shadows. Then the bell clanged, and we crowded again into the stifling dining hall for the last tasteless meal of the barren day. The same miserable stories were told again and again—Colonel Moller's surrender after Talana Hill, and the white flag at Nicholson's Nek—until I knew how the others came to Pretoria as well as I knew my own story.

'We never realised what had happened until we were actually prisoners,' said the officers of the Dublin Fusiliers

Mounted Infantry, who had been captured with Colonel Moller on October 20. 'The "cease fire" sounded: no one knew what had happened. Then we were ordered to form up at the farmhouse, and there we found Boers, who told us to lay down our arms: we were delivered into their hands and never even allowed to have a gallop for freedom. But wait for the Court of Inquiry.'

I used always to sit next to Colonel Carleton at dinner, and from him and from the others learned the story of Nicholson's Nek, which it is not necessary to repeat here, but which filled me with sympathy for the gallant commander and soldiers who were betrayed by the act of an irresponsible subordinate. The officers of the Irish Fusiliers told me of the amazement with which they had seen the white flag flying. 'We had still some ammunition,' they said; 'it is true the position was indefensible—but we only wanted to fight it out.'

'My company was scarcely engaged,' said one poor captain, with tears of vexation in his eyes at the memory; and the Gloucesters told the same tale.

'We saw the hateful thing flying. The firing stopped. No one knew by whose orders the flag had been hoisted. While we doubted the Boers were all among us disarming the men.'

I will write no more upon these painful subjects except to say this, that the hoisting of a white flag in token of surrender is an act which can be justified only by clear proof that there was no prospect of gaining

the slightest military
advantage by going
on fighting; and that
the raising of a white
flag in any case by
an unauthorised
person—i.e. not
the officer in chief
command—in such
a manner as to
compromise the
resistance of a force,
deserves sentence
of death, though
in view of the high
standard of discipline

and honour prevailing in her Majesty's army, it might not be necessary to carry the sentence into effect. I earnestly trust that in justice to gallant officers and soldiers, who have languished these weary months in Pretoria, there will be a strict inquiry into the circumstances under which they became prisoners of war. I have no doubt we shall be told that it is a foolish thing to wash dirty linen in public; but much better wash it in public than wear it foul.

One day shortly after I had arrived I had an interesting visit, for de Souza, wishing to have an argument brought

Mr. Grobelaar to see me. This gentleman was the Under Secretary for Foreign Affairs, and had just returned from Mafeking, whither he had been conducting a 6-inch gun. He was a very well-educated person, and so far as I could tell, honest and capable besides. With him came Reuter's Agent, Mr. Mackay, and the odious Malan. I received them sitting on my bed in the dormitory, and when they had lighted cigars, of which I always kept a stock, we had a regular durbar. I began:

'Well, Mr. Grobelaar, you see how your Government treats representatives of the Press.'

Grobelaar. 'I hope

you have nothing to complain of

Self. 'Look at the sentries with loaded rifles on every side. I might be a wild beast instead of a special correspondent.'

Grobelaar. 'Ah, but putting aside the sentries with loaded rifles, you do not, I trust, Mr. Churchill, make any complaint.'

Self. 'My chief objection to this place is that I am in it.'

Grobelaar. 'That of course is your misfortune, and Mr. Chamberlain's fault.

Self. 'Not at all. We are a peace-loving people, but we had no choice but to fight or be— what was it your burghers told me in the camps?—"driven into the sea." The responsibility of the war is upon you and your President.'

Grobelaar. 'Don't you believe that. We did not want to fight. We only wanted to be left alone.'

Self. 'You never wanted war?'

de Souza. 'Ah, my God, no! Do you

think we would fight Great Britain for amusement?'

Self. 'Then why did you make every preparation—turn the Republics into armed camps—prepare deep-laid plans for the invasion of our Colonies?'

Grobelaar. 'Why, what could we do after the Jameson Raid? We had to be ready to protect ourselves.'

Self. 'Surely less extensive armaments would have been sufficient to guard against another similar inroad.'

Grobelaar. 'But we knew your Government was behind the Raiders. Jameson was in front, but Rhodes and your Colonial Office were at his elbow.'

Self. 'As a matter of fact no two people were more disconcerted by the Raid than Chamberlain and Rhodes. Besides, the British Government disavowed the Raiders' action and punished the Raiders, who, I am quite prepared to admit, got no more than they deserved.'

de Souza. 'I don't complain about the British Government's action at the time of the Raid. Chamberlain behaved very honourably then. But it was afterwards, when Rhodes was not punished, that we knew it was all a farce, and that the British Government was bent on our destruction. When the burghers knew that Rhodes was not punished they lost all trust in England.'

Malan. 'Ya, ya. That Rhodes, he is the ... at the bottom of it all. You wait and see what we will do to Rhodes when we take Kimberley.'

Self. 'Then you maintain, de Souza, that the distrust

caused in this country by the fact that Rhodes was not punished—though how you can punish a man who breaks no law I cannot tell—was the sole cause of your Government making these gigantic military preparations, because it is certain that these preparations were the actual cause of war.'

Grobelaar. 'Why should they be a cause of war? We would never have attacked you.'

Self. 'But at this moment you are invading Cape Colony and Natal, while no British soldier has set foot on Republican soil. Moreover, it was you who declared war upon us.'

Grobelaar. 'Naturally

we were not such fools as to wait till your army was here. As soon as you began to send your army, we were bound to declare war. If you had sent it earlier we should have fought earlier. Really, Mr. Churchill, you must see that is only common sense.'

Self. 'I am not criticising your

policy or tactics. You hated us bitterly—I dare say you had cause to. You made tremendous preparations—I don't say you were wrong—but look at it from our point of view. We saw a declared enemy armed and arming. Against us, and against us alone, could his preparations be directed. It was time we took some precautions: indeed, we were already too late. Surely what has happened at the front proves that we had no designs against you. You were ready. We were unready. It is the wolf and lamb if you like; but the wolf was asleep and never before was a lamb with such teeth and claws.'

Grobelaar. 'Do you really mean to say that we forced this war on you, that you did not want to fight us?'

Self. 'The country did not wish for war with the Boers. Personally, I have always done so. I saw that you had six rifles to every burgher in the Republic. I knew what that meant. It meant that you were going to raise a great Afrikander revolt against us. One does not set extra places at table unless one expects company to dinner. On the other hand, we have affairs all over the world, and at any moment may become embroiled with a European power. At this time things are very quiet. The board is clear in other directions. We can give you our undivided attention. Armed and ambitious as you were, the war had to come sooner or later. I have always said "sooner." Therefore, I rejoiced when you sent your ultimatum and roused the whole nation.'

Malan. 'You don't

rejoice quite so much now.'

Self. 'My opinion is unaltered, except that the necessity for settling the matter has become more apparent.
As for the result, that, as I think Mr. Grobelaar knows, is only a question of time and money expressed in terms of blood and tears.'

Grobelaar. 'No: our opinion is quite unchanged. We prepared for the war. We have always thought we could beat you. We do not doubt our calculations now. We have done better even than we expected. The President is extremely pleased.'

Self. 'There is no

good arguing on that point. We shall have to fight it out. But if you had tried to keep on friendly terms with us, the war would not have come for a long time; and the delay was all on your side.'

Grobelaar. 'We have tried till we are sick of it. This Government was badgered out of its life with Chamberlain's despatches—such despatches. And then look how we have been lied about in your papers, and called barbarians and savages.'

Self. 'I think you have certainly been abused unjustly. Indeed, when I was taken prisoner the other day, I thought it quite possible I should be put to death, although I was a correspondent' (great laughter, 'Fancy that!' etc.). 'At the best I expected to be held in prison as a kind of hostage. See how I have been mistaken.'

I pointed at the sentry who stood in the doorway, for even members of the Government could not visit us alone. Grobelaar flushed. 'Oh, well, we will hope that the captivity will not impair your spirits. Besides, it will not last long. The President expects peace before the New Year.'

'I shall hope to be free by then.'

And with this the

interview came to an end, and my visitors withdrew. The actual conversation had lasted more than an hour, but the dialogue above is not an inaccurate summary.

About ten days after my arrival at Pretoria I received a visit from the American Consul, Mr. Macrum. It seems that

some uncertainty
prevailed at home
as to whether I was
alive, wounded or
unwounded, and
in what light I was
regarded by the
Transvaal authorities.
Mr. Bourke Cockran,
an American Senator
who had long been
a friend of mine,
telegraphed from
New York to the
United States
representative in

Pretoria, hoping by this neutral channel to learn how the case stood. I had not, however, talked with Mr. Macrum for very long before I realised that neither I nor any other British prisoner was likely to be the better for any efforts which he might make on our behalf. His sympathies were plainly so much with the Transvaal Government that he even found it difficult to discharge his diplomatic duties. However, he so far sank his political opinions as to telegraph to Mr. Bourke Cockran, and the anxiety which my relations were suffering on my account was thereby terminated.

I had one other visitor in these dull days, whom I should like to notice. During the afternoon which I spent among the Boers in their camp behind Bulwana Hill I had exchanged a few words with an Englishman whose name is of no consequence, but who was the gunner entrusted with the aiming of the big

6-inch gun. He was a
light-hearted jocular
fellow outwardly,
but I was not long in
discovering that his
anxieties among the
Boers were grave
and numerous. He
had been drawn into
the war, so far as
I could make out,
more by the desire
of sticking to his
own friends and
neighbours than even
of preserving his

property. But besides this local spirit, which counterbalanced the racial and patriotic feelings, there was a very strong desire to be upon the winning side, and I think that he regarded the Boers with an aversion which increased in proportion as their successes fell short of their early anticipations. One afternoon he called at the States Model Schools prison and, being duly authorised to visit the prisoners, asked to see me. In the presence of Dr. Gunning, I had an interesting interview. At first our conversation was confined to generalities, but gradually, as the other officers in the room, with ready tact, drew the little Hollander Professor into an argument, my renegade and I were able to exchange confidences.

I was of course above all things anxious to get true news from the outer world, and whenever Dr. Gunning's attention was distracted by his discussion with the officers, I managed to get a little.

'Well, you know,' said the gunner, 'you English don't play fair at Ladysmith at all. We have allowed you to have a camp at Intombi Spruit for your wounded, and yet we see red cross flags flying in the town, and we have heard that in the Church there is a magazine of ammunition protected by the red cross flag. Major Erasmus, he says to me "John, you smash up that building," and so when I go back I am going to fire into the church.' Gunning broke out into panegyrics on the virtues of the Afrikanders: my companion dropped his voice. 'The Boers have had a terrible beating at Belmont; the Free Staters have lost more than 200 killed; much discouraged; if your people keep on like this the Free State will break up.' He raised his voice, 'Ladysmith hold out a month? Not possible; we shall give it a fortnight's more bombardment, and then you will just see how the burghers will scramble into their trenches. Plenty of whisky then, ha, ha, ha!' Then lower, 'I wish to God I could get away from this, but I don't know what to do; they are always suspecting me and watching me, and I have to keep on pretending I want them to win. This is a terrible position for a man to be in: curse the filthy Dutchmen!'

I said, 'Will Methuen
get to Kimberley?'

'I don't know, but
he gave them hell
at Belmont and
at Graspan, and
they say they are
fighting again to-day
at Modder River.
Major Erasmus is
very down-hearted
about it. But the
ordinary burghers
hear nothing but lies;
all lies, I tell you.

(Crescendo) Look at the lies that have been told about us! Barbarians! savages! every name your papers have called us, but you know better than that now; you know how well we have treated you since you have been a prisoner; and look at the way your people have treated our prisoners—put them on board ship to make them sea-sick! Don't you call that cruel?'

Here Gunning broke in that it was time for visitors to leave the prison. And so my strange guest, a feather blown along by the wind, without character or stability, a renegade, a traitor to his blood and birthplace, a time-server, had to hurry away. I took his measure; nor did his protestations of alarm excite my sympathy, and yet somehow I did not feel unkindly towards him; a weak man is a pitiful object in times of trouble. Some of our countrymen who were living in the Transvaal and the Orange Free State at the outbreak of the war have been placed in such difficult positions and torn by so many conflicting emotions that they must be judged very tolerantly. How few men are strong enough to stand against the prevailing currents of opinion! Nor, after the desertion of the British residents in the Transvaal in 1881, have we the right to judge their successors harshly if they have failed us, for it was Great and Mighty Britain who was the renegade and traitor then.

No sooner had I reached Pretoria than I demanded my release from the Government, on the grounds that I was a Press correspondent and a non-combatant. So many people have found it difficult to reconcile this position with the accounts which have been published of what transpired during the defence of the armoured train, that I am compelled to explain. Besides the soldiers of the Dublin Fusiliers and Durban Light Infantry who had been captured, there were also eight or ten civilians, including a fireman, a telegraphist, and several men of the breakdown gang. Now it seems to me that according to international practice and the customs of war, the Transvaal Government were perfectly justified in regarding all persons connected with a military train as actual combatants; indeed, the fact that they were not soldiers was, if anything, an aggravation of their case. But the Boers were at that time overstocked with prisoners whom they had to feed and guard, and they therefore announced that the civilians would be released as soon as their identity was established, and only the military retained as prisoners.

In my case, however, an exception was to be made, and General Joubert, who had read the gushing accounts of my conduct which appeared in the Natal newspapers, directed that since I had taken part in the fighting I was to be treated as a combatant officer.

Now, as it happened, I had confined myself

strictly to the business of clearing the line, which was entrusted to me, and although I do not pretend that I considered the matter in its legal aspect at the time, the fact remains that I did not give a shot, nor was I armed when captured. I therefore claimed to be included in the same category as the civilian railway officials and men of the breakdown gang, whose declared duty it was to clear the line, pointing out that though my action might differ in degree from theirs, it was of precisely the same character, and that if they were regarded as non-combatants I had a right to be considered a non-combatant too.

To this effect I wrote
two letters, one
to the Secretary
of War and one to
General Joubert; but,
needless to say, I
did not indulge in
much hope of the
result, for I was
firmly convinced that
the Boer authorities
regarded me as a
kind of hostage,
who would make a

pleasing addition
to the collection of
prisoners they were
forming against a
change of fortune. I
therefore continued
to search for a
path of escape; and
indeed it was just as
well that I did so, for
I never received any
answer to either of
my applications while
I was a prisoner,
although I have
since heard that one

arrived by a curious coincidence the very day after I had departed.

While I was looking about for means, and awaiting an opportunity to break out of the Model Schools, I made every preparation to make a graceful exit when the moment should arrive. I gave full instructions to my friends as to what was to be done with my clothes and the effects I had accumulated during my stay; I paid my account to date with the excellent Boshof; cashed a cheque on him for 20l.; changed some of the notes I had always concealed on my person since my capture into gold; and lastly, that there might be no unnecessary unpleasantness, I wrote the following letter to the Secretary of State:

States Model Schools Prison: December 10, 1899.

Sir,—I have the honour to inform you that as I do not consider that your Government have any right to detain me as a military prisoner,

I have decided to escape from your custody. I have every confidence in the arrangements I have made with my friends outside, and I do not therefore expect to have another opportunity of seeing you. I therefore take this occasion to observe that I consider your treatment of prisoners is correct and humane, and that I see no grounds for complaint. When I return to the British lines I will make a public statement to this effect. I have also to thank you personally for your civility to me, and to express the hope that we may meet again at Pretoria before very long, and under different circumstances.

Regretting that I am unable to bid you a more ceremonious or a personal farewell,

I have the honour, to be, Sir,

Your most obedient servant,

WINSTON CHURCHILL.

To Mr. de Souza,

Secretary of War, South African Republic.

I arranged that this letter, which I took great pleasure in writing, should be left on my bed, and discovered so soon as my flight was known.

It only remained now to find a hat. Luckily for me Mr. Adrian Hofmeyr, a Dutch clergyman and pastor of Zeerust, had ventured before the war to express opinions contrary to those which the Boers thought befitting for a Dutchman to hold. They had therefore seized him on the outbreak of hostilities, and after much ill-treatment and many indignities on the Western border, brought him to the States Schools. He knew most of the officials, and could, I think, easily have obtained his liberty had he pretended to be in sympathy with the Republics. He was, however, a true man, and after the clergyman of the Church of England, who was rather a poor creature, omitted to read the prayer for the Queen one Sunday, it was to Hofmeyr's evening services alone that most of the officers would go. I borrowed his hat.

I ESCAPE FROM THE BOERS

Lourenço Marques: December 22, 1899,

How unhappy is that poor man who loses his liberty! What can the wide world give him in exchange? No degree of material comfort, no consciousness of correct behaviour, can balance the hateful degradation of imprisonment. Before I had been an hour in captivity, as the previous pages evidence, I resolved to escape. Many plans suggested themselves, were examined, and rejected. For a month I thought of nothing else. But the peril and difficulty restrained action. I think that it was the report of the British defeat at Stormberg that clinched the matter. All the news we heard in Pretoria was derived from Boer sources, and was hideously exaggerated and distorted. Every

day we read in
the 'Volksstem'—
probably the most
astounding tissue of
lies ever presented
to the public under
the name of a
newspaper—of Boer
victories and of the
huge slaughters and
shameful flights
of the British.
However much one
might doubt and
discount these
tales, they made

a deep impression. A month's feeding on such literary garbage weakens the constitution of the mind. We wretched prisoners lost heart. Perhaps Great Britain would not persevere; perhaps Foreign Powers would intervene; perhaps there would be another disgraceful, cowardly peace. At the best the war and our confinement would be prolonged for many months. I do not pretend that impatience at being locked up was not the foundation of my determination; but I should never have screwed up my courage to make the attempt without the earnest desire to do something, however small, to help the British cause. Of course, I am a man of peace. I did not then contemplate becoming an officer of Irregular Horse. But swords are not the only weapons in the world. Something may be done with a pen. So I determined to take all hazards; and, indeed, the affair was one of very great danger and difficulty.

The States Model Schools stand in the midst of a quadrangle, and are surrounded on two sides by an iron grille and on two by a corrugated iron fence about 10 ft. high. These boundaries offered little obstacle to anyone who possessed the activity of youth, but the fact that they were guarded on the inside by sentries, fifty yards apart, armed with rifle and revolver, made them a well-nigh insuperable barrier. No walls are so hard to pierce as living walls. I thought of the penetrating power of gold, and the sentries were sounded. They were incorruptible. I seek not to deprive them of the credit, but the truth is that the bribery market in the Transvaal has been spoiled by the millionaires. I could not afford with my slender resources to insult them heavily enough. So nothing remained but to break out in spite of them. With another officer who may for the present—since he is still a prisoner— remain nameless, I formed a scheme.

After anxious reflection and continual watching, it was discovered that when the sentries near the offices walked about on their beats they were at certain moments unable to see the top of a few yards of the wall. The electric lights in the middle of the

quadrangle brilliantly
lighted the whole
place but cut off
the sentries beyond
them from looking
at the eastern wall,
for from behind the
lights all seemed
darkness by contrast.
The first thing was
therefore to pass
the two sentries
near the offices. It
was necessary to
hit off the exact
moment when both

their backs should be turned together. After the wall was scaled we should be in the garden of the villa next door. There our plan came to an end. Everything after this was vague and uncertain. How to get out of the garden, how to pass unnoticed through the streets, how to evade the patrols that surrounded the town, and above all how to cover the two hundred and eighty miles to the Portuguese frontiers, were questions which would arise at a later stage. All attempts to communicate with friends outside had failed. We cherished the hope that with chocolate, a little Kaffir knowledge, and a great deal of luck, we might march the distance in a fortnight, buying mealies at the native kraals and lying hidden by day. But it did not look a very promising prospect.

We determined to try on the night of the 11th of December, making up our minds quite suddenly in the morning, for these things are best done on the spur of the moment. I passed the afternoon in positive terror. Nothing, since my schooldays, has ever disturbed me so much as this. There is something appalling in the idea of stealing secretly off in the night like a guilty thief. The fear of detection has a pang of its own. Besides, we knew quite well that on occasion, even on excuse, the sentries would fire. Fifteen yards is a short range. And beyond the immediate danger lay a prospect of severe hardship and suffering, only faint hopes of success, and the probability at the best of five months in Pretoria Gaol.

The afternoon dragged tediously

away. I tried to read Mr. Lecky's 'History of England,' but for the first time in my life that wise writer wearied me. I played chess and was hopelessly beaten. At last it grew dark. At seven o'clock the bell for dinner rang and the officers trooped off. Now was the time. But the sentries gave us no chance. They did not walk about. One of them stood exactly opposite the only practicable part of the wall. We waited for two hours, but the attempt was plainly impossible, and so with a most unsatisfactory feeling of relief to bed.

Tuesday, the 12th! Another day of fear, but fear crystallising more and more into desperation. Anything was better than further suspense. Night came again. Again the dinner bell sounded. Choosing my opportunity I strolled across the quadrangle and secreted myself in one of the offices. Through a chink I watched the sentries. For half an hour they remained stolid and obstructive. Then all of a sudden one turned and walked up to his comrade and they began to talk. Their backs were turned. Now or never. I darted out of my hiding place and ran to the wall, seized the top with my hands and drew myself up. Twice I let myself down again in sickly hesitation, and then with a third resolve scrambled up. The top was flat. Lying on it I had one parting glimpse of the sentries, still talking, still with their backs turned; but, I repeat, fifteen yards away. Then I lowered myself silently down into the adjoining garden and crouched among the shrubs. I was free. The first step had been taken, and it was irrevocable.

It now remained to await the arrival of my comrade. The bushes of the garden gave a good deal of cover, and in the moonlight their shadows lay black on the ground. Twenty yards away was the house, and I had not been five minutes in hiding before I perceived that it was full of people; the windows revealed brightly lighted rooms, and within I could see figures moving about. This was a fresh complication. We had always thought the house unoccupied. Presently—how long afterwards I do not know, for the ordinary measures of time, hours, minutes, and seconds are quite meaningless on such occasions—a man came out of the door and walked across the garden in my direction. Scarcely ten yards away he stopped and stood still, looking steadily towards me. I cannot describe the surge of panic which nearly overwhelmed me. I must be discovered.

I dared not stir an inch. My heart beat so violently that I felt sick. But amid a tumult of emotion, reason, seated firmly on her throne, whispered, 'Trust to the dark background.' I remained absolutely motionless. For a long time the man and I remained opposite each other, and every instant I expected him to spring forward. A vague idea crossed my mind that I might silence him. 'Hush, I am a detective. We expect that an officer will break out here to-night. I am waiting to catch him.' Reason—scornful this time—replied: 'Surely a Transvaal detective would speak Dutch. Trust to the shadow.' So I trusted, and after a spell another man came out of the house, lighted a cigar, and both he and the other walked off together. No sooner had they turned than a cat pursued by a dog rushed into the bushes and collided with me. The startled animal uttered a 'miaul' of alarm and darted back again, making a horrible rustling. Both men stopped at once. But it was only the cat, as they doubtless observed, and they passed out of the garden gate into the town.

I looked at my watch. An hour had passed since I climbed the wall. Where was my comrade? Suddenly I heard a voice from within the quadrangle say, quite loud, 'All up.' I crawled back to the wall. Two officers were walking up and down the other side jabbering Latin words, laughing and talking all manner of nonsense—amid which I caught my name. I risked a cough. One of the officers immediately began to chatter alone. The other said slowly and clearly, '... cannot get out. The sentry suspects.

It's all up. Can you get back again?' But now all my fears fell from me at once. To go back was impossible. I could not hope to climb the wall unnoticed. Fate pointed onwards. Besides, I said to myself, 'Of course, I shall be recaptured, but I will at least have a run for my money.' I said to the officers, 'I shall go on alone.'

Now I was in the right mood for these undertakings—that is to say that, thinking failure almost certain, no odds against success affected me. All risks were less than the certainty. A glance at the plan (p. 182) will show that the rate which led into the road was only a few yards from another sentry. I said to myself, 'Toujours de l'audace:' put my hat on my head, strode into the middle of the garden, walked past the windows of the house without any attempt at concealment, and so went through the gate and turned to the left. I passed the sentry at less than five yards. Most of them knew me by sight. Whether he looked at me or not I do not know, for I never turned my head. But after walking a hundred yards and hearing no challenge, I knew that the second obstacle had been surmounted. I was at large in Pretoria.

I walked on leisurely through the night

humming a tune and choosing the middle of the road. The streets were full of Burghers, but they paid no attention to me. Gradually I reached the suburbs, and on a little bridge I sat down to reflect and consider. I was in the heart of the enemy's country. I knew no one to whom I could apply for succour. Nearly

three hundred miles
stretched between
me and Delagoa Bay.
My escape must
be known at dawn.
Pursuit would be
immediate. Yet all
exits were barred.
The town was
picketed, the country
was patrolled, the
trains were searched,
the line was guarded.
I had 75l. in my
pocket and four
slabs of chocolate,

but the compass and the map which might have guided me, the opium tablets and meat lozenges which should have sustained me, were in my friend's pockets in the States Model Schools. Worst of all, I could not speak a word of Dutch or Kaffir, and how was I to get food or direction?

But when hope
had departed, fear
had gone as well.
I formed a plan.
I would find the
Delagoa Bay Railway.
Without map or
compass I must
follow that in spite
of the pickets. I
looked at the stars.
Orion shone brightly.
Scarcely a year ago
he had guided me
when lost in the
desert to the banks

of the Nile. He had given me water. Now he should lead to freedom. I could not endure the want of either.

After walking south for half a mile, I struck the railroad. Was it the line to Delagoa Bay or the Pietersburg branch? If it were the former it should run east. But so far as I could see this line ran northwards. Still, it might be only winding its way out among the hills. I resolved to follow it. The night was delicious. A cool breeze fanned my face and a wild feeling of exhilaration took hold of me. At any rate, I was free, if only for an hour. That was something. The fascination of

the adventure grew.
Unless the stars in
their courses fought
for me I could not
escape. Where, then,
was the need of
caution? I marched
briskly along the
line. Here and there
the lights of a
picket fire gleamed.
Every bridge had
its watchers. But
I passed them
all, making very
short detours at

the dangerous places, and really taking scarcely any precautions. Perhaps that was the reason I succeeded.

As I walked I extended my plan. I could not march three hundred miles to the frontier. I would board a train in motion and hide under the seats, on the roof, on the couplings—anywhere. What train should I take? The first, of course. After walking for two hours I perceived the signal lights of a station. I left the line, and, circling round it, hid in the ditch by the track about 200 yards beyond it. I argued that the train would stop at the station and that it would not have got up too much speed by the time it reached me. An hour passed. I began to grow impatient. Suddenly I heard the whistle and the approaching rattle. Then the great yellow head lights of the engine flashed into view. The train waited five minutes at the station and started again with much noise and steaming. I crouched by the track. I rehearsed the act in my mind. I must wait until the engine had passed, otherwise I should be seen. Then I must make a dash for the carriages.

The train started slowly, but gathered speed sooner than I had expected. The flaring lights drew swiftly near. The rattle grew into a roar. The dark mass hung for a second above me. The engine-driver silhouetted against his furnace glow, the black profile of the engine, the clouds of steam rushed past. Then I hurled myself on the trucks, clutched at something, missed, clutched again, missed again, grasped some sort of hand-hold, was swung off my feet—my toes bumping on the line, and with a struggle seated myself on the couplings of the fifth truck from the front of the train. It was a goods train, and the trucks were full of sacks, soft sacks covered with coal dust. I crawled on top and burrowed in among them. In

five minutes I was
completely buried.
The sacks were warm
and comfortable.
Perhaps the engine-
driver had seen me
rush up to the train
and would give the
alarm at the next
station: on the
other hand, perhaps
not. Where was
the train going to?
Where would it be
unloaded? Would it
be searched? Was it

on the Delagoa Bay line? What should I do in the morning? Ah, never mind that. Sufficient for the day was the luck thereof. Fresh plans for fresh contingencies. I resolved to sleep, nor can I imagine a more pleasing lullaby than the clatter of the train that carries you at twenty miles an hour away from the enemy's capital.

How long I slept I
do not know, but I
woke up suddenly
with all feelings
of exhilaration
gone, and only the
consciousness of
oppressive difficulties
heavy on me. I
must leave the train
before daybreak, so
that I could drink at
a pool and find some
hiding-place while
it was still dark.
Another night I would

board another train.
I crawled from my
cosy hiding-place
among the sacks
and sat again on
the couplings. The
train was running at
a fair speed, but I
felt it was time to
leave it. I took hold
of the iron handle
at the back of the
truck, pulled strongly
with my left hand,
and sprang. My feet
struck the ground in

two gigantic strides, and the next instant I was sprawling in the ditch, considerably shaken but unhurt. The train, my faithful ally of the night, hurried on its journey.

It was still dark. I was in the middle of a wide valley, surrounded by low hills, and carpeted with high grass drenched in dew. I searched for water in the nearest gully, and soon found a clear pool. I was very thirsty, but long after I had quenched my thirst I continued to drink, that I might have sufficient for the whole day.

Presently the dawn began to break, and the sky to the east grew yellow and red, slashed across with heavy black clouds. I saw with relief that the railway ran steadily towards the sunrise. I had taken the right line, after all.

Having drunk my fill, I set out for the hills, among which I hoped to find some hiding-place, and as it became broad daylight I entered a small grove of trees which grew on the side of a deep ravine. Here I resolved to wait till dusk. I had one consolation: no one in the world knew where I was—I did not know myself. It was now four o'clock. Fourteen hours lay between me and the night. My impatience to proceed, while I was still strong, doubled their length. At first it was terribly cold, but by degrees the sun gained power, and by ten o'clock the heat was oppressive. My sole companion was a gigantic vulture, who manifested an extravagant interest in my condition, and made hideous and ominous gurglings from time to time. From my lofty position I commanded a view of the whole valley. A little tin-roofed town lay three miles to the westward. Scattered farmsteads, each with a clump of trees, relieved the monotony of the undulating ground. At the foot of the hill stood a Kaffir kraal, and the figures of its inhabitants dotted the patches of cultivation or surrounded the droves of goats and cows which fed on the pasture. The railway ran through the middle of the valley, and I could watch the passage of the various trains. I counted four passing each way, and from this I drew the conclusion that the same number would run by night. I marked a steep gradient up which they climbed very slowly, and determined at nightfall to make another attempt to board one of these. During the day I ate one slab of chocolate, which, with the heat, produced a violent thirst. The pool was hardly half a mile away, but I dared not leave the shelter of the little wood, for I could see the figures of white men riding or walking occasionally across the valley, and once a Boer came and fired two shots at birds close to my hiding-place. But no one discovered me.

The elation and the excitement of the previous night had

burnt away, and a chilling reaction followed. I was very hungry, for I had had no dinner before starting, and chocolate, though it sustains, does not satisfy. I had scarcely slept, but yet my heart beat so fiercely and I was so nervous and perplexed about the future that I could not rest. I thought

of all the chances
that lay against
me; I dreaded and
detested more than
words can express
the prospect of being
caught and dragged
back to Pretoria. I
do not mean that I
would rather have
died than have been
retaken, but I have
often feared death
for much less. I found
no comfort in any
of the philosophical

ideas which some men parade in their hours of ease and strength and safety. They seemed only fair-weather friends. I realised with awful force that no exercise of my own feeble wit and strength could save me from my enemies, and that without the assistance of that High Power which interferes in the eternal sequence of causes and effects more often than we are always prone to admit, I could never succeed. I prayed long and earnestly for help and guidance. My prayer, as it seems to me, was swiftly and wonderfully answered, I cannot now relate the strange circumstances which followed, and which changed my nearly hopeless position into one of superior advantage. But after the war is over I shall hope to lengthen this account, and so remarkable will the addition be that I cannot believe the reader will complain.

The long day reached its close at last. The western clouds

flushed into fire; the shadows of the hills stretched out across the valley. A ponderous Boer waggon, with its long team, crawled slowly along the track towards the town. The Kaffirs collected their herds and drew around their kraal. The daylight died, and soon it was quite dark. Then, and not till then, I set forth, I hurried to the railway line, pausing on my way to drink at a stream of sweet, cold water. I waited for some time at the top of the steep gradient in the hope of catching a train. But none came, and I gradually guessed, and I have since found that I guessed right, that the train I had already travelled in was the only one

that ran at night.
At last I resolved to
walk on, and make,
at any rate, twenty
miles of my journey.
I walked for about
six hours. How far
I travelled I do not
know, but I do not
think that it was
very many miles in
the direct line. Every
bridge was guarded
by armed men; every
few miles were
gangers' huts; at

intervals there were stations with villages clustering round them. All the veldt was bathed in the bright rays of the full moon, and to avoid these dangerous places I had to make wide circuits and often to creep along the ground. Leaving the railroad I fell into bogs and swamps, and brushed through high grass dripping with dew, so that I was drenched to the waist. I had been able to take little exercise during my month's imprisonment, and I was soon tired out with walking, as well as from want of food and sleep. I felt very miserable when I looked around and saw here and there the lights of houses, and thought of the warmth and comfort within them, but knew that they only meant danger to me. After six or seven hours of walking I thought it unwise to go further lest I should exhaust myself, so I lay down in a ditch to sleep. I was nearly at the end of my tether. Nevertheless, by the will of God, I was enabled to sustain myself during the next few days, obtaining food at great risk here and there, resting in concealment by day and walking only at night. On the fifth day I was beyond Middelburg, so far as I could tell, for I dared not inquire nor as yet approach the stations near enough to read the names. In a secure hiding-place I waited for a suitable train, knowing that there is a through service between Middelburg and Lourenço Marques.

Meanwhile there had been excitement in the States Model Schools, temporarily converted into a military prison. Early on Wednesday morning—barely twelve hours after

I had escaped—
my absence was
discovered—I think
by Dr. Gunning. The
alarm was given.
Telegrams with
my description at
great length were
despatched along
all the railways.
Three thousand
photographs were
printed. A warrant
was issued for my
immediate arrest.
Every train was

strictly searched. Everyone was on the watch. The worthy Boshof, who knew my face well, was hurried off to Komati Poort to examine all and sundry people "with red hair" travelling towards the frontier. The newspapers made so much of the affair that my humble fortunes and my whereabouts were discussed in long columns of print, and even in the crash of the war I became to the Boers a topic all to myself. The rumours in part amused me. It was certain, said the "Standard and Diggers' News," that I had escaped disguised as a woman. The next day I was reported captured at Komati

Poort dressed as a Transvaal policeman. There was great delight at this, which was only changed to doubt when other telegrams said that I had been arrested at Brugsbank, at Middelburg, and at Bronkerspruit. But the captives proved to be harmless people after all. Finally it was agreed that I had never left

Pretoria. I had—it appeared—changed clothes with a waiter, and was now in hiding at the house of some British sympathiser in the capital. On the strength of this all the houses of suspected persons were searched from top to bottom, and these unfortunate people were, I fear, put to a great deal of inconvenience. A special commission was also appointed to investigate 'stringently' (a most hateful adjective in such a connection) the causes 'which had rendered it possible for the War Correspondent of the "Morning Post" to escape.'

The 'Volksstem' noticed as a significant fact

that I had recently become a subscriber to the State Library, and had selected Mill's essay 'On Liberty.' It apparently desired to gravely deprecate prisoners having access to such inflammatory literature. The idea will, perhaps, amuse those who have read the work in question.

I find it very difficult

in the face of the extraordinary efforts which were made to recapture me, to believe that the Transvaal Government seriously contemplated my release before they knew I had escaped them. Yet a telegram was swiftly despatched from Pretoria to all the newspapers, setting forth the terms of a most admirable letter, in which General Joubert explained the grounds which prompted him generously to restore my liberty. I am inclined to think that the Boers hate being beaten even in the smallest things, and always fight on the win, tie, or wrangle principle; but in my case I rejoice I am not beholden to them, and have not thus been disqualified from fighting.

All these things may provoke a smile of indifference, perhaps even of triumph, after the danger is past; but during the days when I was lying up in holes and corners, waiting for a good chance to board a train, the causes

that had led to them
preyed more than I
knew on my nerves.
To be an outcast,
to be hunted, to
lie under a warrant
for arrest, to fear
every man, to have
imprisonment—not
necessarily military
confinement either—
hanging overhead, to
fly the light, to doubt
the shadows—all
these things ate into
my soul and have left

an impression that will not perhaps be easily effaced.

On the sixth day the chance I had patiently waited for came. I found a convenient train duly labelled to Lourenço Marques standing in a siding. I withdrew to a suitable spot for boarding it—for I dared not make the attempt in the station—and, filling a bottle with water to drink on the way, I prepared for the last stage of my journey.

The truck in which I ensconced myself was laden with great sacks of some soft merchandise, and I found among them holes and crevices by means of which I managed to work my way to the inmost recess. The hard floor was littered with gritty coal dust, and made a most uncomfortable bed. The heat was almost stifling. I was resolved, however, that nothing should lure or compel me from my hiding-place until I reached Portuguese territory. I expected the journey to take thirty-six hours; it dragged out into two and a half days. I hardly dared sleep for fear of snoring.

I dreaded lest the trucks should be searched at Komati Poort, and my anxiety as the train approached this neighbourhood was very great. To prolong it we were shunted on to a siding for eighteen hours either at Komati Poort or the station beyond it. Once indeed they began to search my truck, and I heard the tarpaulin rustle as they pulled at it, but luckily they did not search deep enough, so that, providentially protected, I reached Delagoa Bay at last, and crawled forth from my place of refuge and of punishment, weary, dirty, hungry, but free once more.

Thereafter everything smiled. I found my way to the British Consul, Mr. Ross, who at first mistook me for a fireman off one of the ships in the harbour, but soon welcomed me with enthusiasm.

I bought clothes, I washed, I sat down to dinner with a real tablecloth and real glasses; and fortune, determined not to overlook the smallest detail, had arranged that the steamer 'Induna' should leave that very night for Durban. As soon as the news of my arrival spread about the town, I received many offers of assistance from the English residents, and lest any of the Boer agents with whom Lourenço Marques is infested should attempt to recapture me in neutral territory, nearly a dozen gentlemen escorted me to the steamer armed with revolvers. It is from the cabin of this little vessel, as she coasts along the sandy shores of Africa, that I write the concluding lines of this letter, and the reader who may persevere through this hurried account will perhaps understand why I write them with a feeling of triumph, and better than triumph, a feeling of pure joy.

ABOUT THE AUTHOR

Winston Churchill's hunt for fame and glory had already taken him to India and Cuba when he went to South Africa to cover the Boer War for the Morning Post. His capture, and the manhunt that followed his escape was big news and helped him get elected to the Parliament.

ABOUT THE COVER

The image on the cover is adapted from a photo of a 26 year old Winston Churchill on a lecture tour of the United States in 1900.

MORE BOOKS AT:
superlargeprint.com
KEEP ON READING!

This book is set in a font designed by
Abelardo Gonzalez called OpenDyslexic.

ISBN 9781092125079

Made in the USA
Monee, IL
16 September 2019